EVERYTHING
THE BIBLE SAYS
ABOUT
PARENTING
& CHILDREN

EVERYTHING THE BIBLE SAYS ABOUT

PARENTING & CHILDREN

BETHANY HOUSE PUBLISHERS

a division of Baker Publishing Group
Minneapolis, Minnesota

© 2012 by Bethany House Publishers

Compiled by Aaron Sharp
Series editor: Andy McGuire

Published by Bethany House Publishers
11400 Hampshire Avenue South
Bloomington, Minnesota 55438
www.bethanyhouse.com

Bethany House Publishers is a division of
Baker Publishing Group, Grand Rapids, Michigan

Printed in the United States of America

Library of Congress Cataloging-in-Publication Data
Everything the Bible says about parenting and children / [compiled by Aaron Sharp].
   p.   cm.
   Summary: All the key Bible references concerning parents and children, including instruction and examples of biblical families"—Provided by publisher.
   "How does God show his love for children? How can I raise my children to know right from wrong? How should I teach my children about God? What does the Bible say about discipline?."
   Includes bibliographical references (p.   ).
   ISBN 978-0-7642-0989-5 (pbk. : alk. paper)
   1. Parenting—Religious aspects—Christianity. 2. Child rearing—Religious aspects—Christianity. 3. Parenting—Biblical teaching. 4. Child rearing—Biblical teaching. 5. Bible—Quotations. I. Sharp, Aaron.
BV4529.E94 2012
248.8'45—dc23   2012013960

Cover design by Eric Walljasper

12 13 14 15 16 17 18   7 6 5 4 3 2 1

Contents

Introduction

If there is one activity that has the capability of bringing the bravest and noblest of people to their knees, it is parenting. Bookstores are full of parenting manuals, sermons exhort wise parenting, and television talk shows portray families of every type. Yet as comedian Bill Cosby says, "In spite of the six thousand manuals on child-raising in the bookstores, child-raising is still a dark continent and no one really knows anything."[1] Cosby's words reflect emotions that many parents have felt. Mankind has put men on the moon and sent mechanical rovers to Mars, but the best method for raising a child can often seem as elusive as winning the lottery.

Mankind has been raising children for thousands of years, yet almost every parent can identify with the words of John Wilmot, the Earl of Rochester in the seventeenth century: "Before I got married I had six theories about bringing up children; now I have six children and no theories."[2] Thankfully, for those who feel that parenting can be a black hole where good intentions and wisdom disappear, never to return, there is one book whose wisdom is infallible: the Bible. With its pages of divine writing, the Bible promises wisdom about parenting and children straight from the Almighty himself.

1

What God Expects From Parents

〜〜〜

He who thinks it easy to bring up a family never had one of his own. A mother who trains her children aright had need be wiser than Solomon, for his son turned out a fool.

Charles Haddon Spurgeon[3]

The Bible is far more than a list of things to do and not do, but its pages certainly contain plenty of commands and prohibitions for mankind in general and for specific groups in particular. There are detailed instructions for priests, kings, prophets, disciples, husbands, and wives, to name a few. But the pages of Scripture also include many and varied commands and instructions for parents.

Throughout history, the divine decrees of Scripture to parents have been followed by some and ignored by others.

Yet despite mankind's frequent failure to follow the Bible's timeless wisdom for parents, God's instructions and expectations for parents are as current and practical as anything that you will read on the subject.

Then Esau looked at the women and children and asked, "Who are these people with you?" "These are the children God has graciously given to me, your servant," Jacob replied. **(GENESIS 33:5 NLT)**

> *As a husband and a father, the Old Testament patriarch Jacob was a deeply flawed man, but even he was able to recognize that children are a gift to parents from God.*

And that you may tell in the hearing of your son, and of your grandson, how I made a mockery of the Egyptians and how I performed My signs among them, that you may know that I am the LORD. **(EXODUS 10:2 NASB)**

> *This command, given by God through Moses to the Israelites who were in slavery in Egypt, coincided with the eighth of ten plagues that God sent to punish the Egyptians, which caused Pharaoh to release them from slavery. This eighth plague consisted of massive swarms of locusts that destroyed much of the Egyptians' crops and trees.*

Just make sure you stay alert. Keep close watch over yourselves. Don't forget anything of what you've seen. Don't let your heart wander off. Stay vigilant as long as you live. Teach what you've seen and heard to your children and grandchildren. **(DEUTERONOMY 4:9 THE MESSAGE)**

The role of a parent is one that requires constant vigilance, over both the child and the life of the parent. Not only must parents teach God's Word and ways to their children and grandchildren, but they must also follow them.

Fix these words of mine in your hearts and minds; tie them as symbols on your hands and bind them on your foreheads. Teach them to your children, talking about them when you sit at home and when you walk along the road, when you lie down and when you get up. Write them on the doorframes of your houses and on your gates, so that your days and the days of your children may be many in the land the LORD swore to give your ancestors, as many as the days that the heavens are above the earth. (DEUTERONOMY 11:18-21 NIV)

The book of Deuteronomy is a collection of Moses' final instructions to the nation of Israel before they would enter the Promised Land. The parents of ancient Israel were instructed to consistently and intentionally teach God's Word to their children, keeping those words always before them.

Moses came and recited all the words of this song in the hearing of the people, he and Joshua son of Nun. When Moses had finished saying all these words to all Israel, he said, "Take to heart all these words to which I give witness today and urgently command your children to put them into practice, every single word of this Revelation. Yes. This is no small matter for you; it's your life. In keeping this word you'll have a good and long life in this land that you're crossing the Jordan to possess" (DEUTERONOMY 32:44-47 THE MESSAGE).

Moses' words here were some of his last words to the nation of Israel, which he led for several decades. The pattern that he set forth for the nation of Israel here is for parents to act as commanded by the Word of God, and for children to follow suit acting as directed by the Word of God.

Lo, children are an heritage of the LORD: and the fruit of the womb is his reward **(PSALM 127:3 KJV)**

The Hebrew word Nachalah, which is translated "heritage" here, was also used of a piece of property or land that was given by one person to a succeeding generation.

Only the living can praise you as I do today. Each generation tells of your faithfulness to the next. **(ISAIAH 38:19 NLT)**

When King Hezekiah was healed of a terminal illness by God, he sang a song of thanksgiving to God for healing him. In the midst of this song, he proclaimed that fathers are to teach their children God's truth.

Listen, dear friends, to God's truth, bend your ears to what I tell you. I'm chewing on the morsel of a proverb; I'll let you in on the sweet old truths, Stories we heard from our fathers, counsel we learned at our mother's knee. We're not keeping this to ourselves, we're passing it along to the next generation—God's fame and fortune, the marvelous things he has done. **(PSALM 78:1–4 THE MESSAGE)**

Just as a father has compassion on his children, So the LORD has compassion on those who fear Him. **(PSALM 103:13 NASB)**

Parents are to be the first examples to their children of the character and qualities of God. Parents, and particularly fathers, are to exhibit compassion to their children and not harshness.

He who withholds his rod hates his son, But he who loves him disciplines him diligently. **(PROVERBS 13:24 NASB)**

Discipline your son, for there is hope; do not set your heart on putting him to death. **(PROVERBS 19:18 ESV)**

Children must be disciplined while there is opportunity, for there will come a day when it is too late for a parent's discipline to do any good. For a parent not to discipline their child is to allow them to continue in ways of folly, which puts them on a path to their eventual death.

Do not withhold discipline from a child; if you punish them with the rod, they will not die. Punish them with the rod and save them from death. **(PROVERBS 23:13–14 NIV)**

Of all the verses in the Bible regarding parents, children, and the dispensing of discipline, this verse in Proverbs is probably the most controversial and disconcerting to students of the Scriptures. Much of the consternation stems from the original King James Version's translation of punish *as "beat." Modern versions, such as the NIV seen here, translate the word* nakah *as "punish" to clarify that this verse teaches discipline, but nowhere in the Bible do its pages encourage, or even allow, for discipline that crosses the line into abuse. Here, King Solomon again asserts that children who are allowed to grow up without discipline will face a treacherous life for which they are unprepared.*

The rod and reproof give wisdom, but a child left to himself brings shame to his mother. . . . Discipline your son, and he will give you rest; he will give delight to your heart. **(PROVERBS 29:15, 17 ESV)**

The purpose of disciplining a child as given in this verse is to instill and build wisdom. When that kind of wise discipline is given, that child will be a delight to their parents; but if that kind of discipline is lacking, there will instead be shame at that child's discipline-lacking words and actions.

Train up a child in the way he should go [and in keeping with his individual gift or bent], and when he is old he will not depart from it. **(PROVERBS 22:6 AMP)**

Often this verse has been viewed as suggesting that if a child is trained, disciplined, and discipled properly as a child, they will not stray from their faith. This has led many honest and sincere parents to feel guilty when their children make poor choices as adults. Scholars, however, generally view the verse as having one of two meanings. First, children are to be trained as the habit or nature of the child (such as the age and manner of child) dictate. Second, children are to be trained according to the habit or nature that each individual child displays during their youth.

Tell your children about it in the years to come, and let your children tell their children. Pass the story down from generation to generation. **(JOEL 1:3 NLT)**

Fathers, do not provoke your children to anger, but bring them up in the discipline and instruction of the LORD. (EPHE-SIANS 6:4 ESV)

The Greek word parorgizo, *which is translated "provoke," speaks of someone's actions angering another to the point of exasperation. Often the word is used to speak of the extent to which mankind's sin provokes God. At issue here is not that fathers are never to anger their children, but that their style of parenting and relating to their children is not one that is adversarial and that leaves their children constantly exasperated and with a broken spirit. Instead of operating as an adversary to their children, fathers are to focus on motivating them and nurturing them to be disciplined and knowledgeable followers of Christ.*

Fathers, do not provoke your children, lest they become discouraged. (COLOSSIANS 3:21 NKJV)

The books of Colossians and Ephesians are very similar New Testament epistles. Both books were written by the apostle Paul, and many scholars believe that they were written around the same time, while Paul was in prison in Rome. Because of this, the two books share many common themes, and in fact many of the verses in the two letters are very similar. Just as he did in Ephesians, here in Colossians, Paul urges fathers in particular not to provoke their children, because if they do, they could cause their children to lose heart and become discouraged. Discipline that is enacted too harshly or too severely will be almost as ineffective as no discipline. A child that is constantly provoked will be discouraged and broken.

People who don't take care of their relatives, and especially their own families, have given up their faith. They are worse than someone who doesn't have faith in the LORD. (1 TIMOTHY 5:8 CEV)

As incredible as it may seem, not every parent adequately takes care of their children. It is the role and purpose of parents to take care of their children's spiritual, mental, and physical well-being. To fail to take care of your family is to live a life without faith in God.

Older women likewise are to be reverent in their behavior, not malicious gossips nor enslaved to much wine, teaching what is good, so that they may encourage the young women to love their husbands, to love their children. (TITUS 2:3–4 NASB)

Just as it can seem incredible that some parents need to be told to take care of their children's needs, it is somewhat more incredible that the command needs to be given for mothers to love their children. Yet the love of a child requires a type of sacrifice that is contrary to the nature of fallen human beings, which is why it is so important that parents look to older examples of love and emulate it.

You must submit to and endure [correction] for discipline; God is dealing with you as with sons. For what son is there whom his father does not [thus] train and correct and discipline? (HEBREWS 12:7 AMP)

The pattern of consistently and diligently instilling discipline in children is not one that God simply expects from parents; it is one after which he exemplifies and patterns his own fatherhood.

Behold, the third time I am ready to come to you; and I will not be burdensome to you: for I seek not yours but you: for the children ought not to lay up for the parents, but the parents for the children. **(2 CORINTHIANS 12:14 KJV)**

The apostle Paul says that his pattern of supporting himself rather than relying on support from his spiritual children was based upon the principle that parents are to provide for and support their children.

2

How Parents Affect
Their Children

We hear a great deal about the rudeness of the rising generation. I am an oldster myself and might be expected to take the oldster's side, but in fact I have been far more impressed by the bad manners of parents to children than by those of children to parents. Who has not been the embarrassed guest at family meals where the father or mother treated their grown-up offspring with an incivility which, offered to any other young people, would simply have terminated the acquaintance?[4]

C. S. Lewis

Not everyone has the same reaction when they hear the words *mom* or *dad*. There are those who think of their parents fondly, the memories of their childhood bringing a smile to their face. But there are also those who think sadly upon their parents, and thoughts of their childhood bring tears to their eyes. The relationship that a child has with his or her parents can be a blessed and wonderful thing, or it can give a child immense amounts of baggage and issues.

In truth, there are no perfect parents. Good parents, even according to God's standards, are flawed, just as their parents were before them. And even dishonorable parents can have moments and periods where they truly love their children and seek their best interests. Rather than merely drawing a line between honorable parents and dishonorable parents, the Bible instead communicates to us principles of parenting, as well as showing us the impact that applying or not applying those principles has on parents, children, and the world.

For I have chosen him, so that he may command his children and his household after him to keep the way of the LORD by doing righteousness and justice, so that the LORD may bring upon Abraham what He has spoken about him. (GENESIS 18:19 NASB)

Abraham was called of God to do many things in his life, but one of the most important is found in this verse. Abraham was to set the bar high as a parent by directing and teaching his children to follow God and his ways.

One day Sarah saw the son that Hagar the Egyptian had borne to Abraham, poking fun at her son Isaac. She told Abraham, "Get rid of this slave woman and her son. No child of this slave is going to share inheritance with my son Isaac!"

The matter gave great pain to Abraham—after all, Ishmael was his son. But God spoke to Abraham, "Don't feel badly about the boy and your maid. Do whatever Sarah tells you. Your descendants will come through Isaac. Regarding your maid's son, be assured that I'll also develop a great nation from him—he's your son, too."

Abraham got up early the next morning, got some food together and a canteen of water for Hagar, put them on her back and sent her away with the child. She wandered off into the desert of Beersheba. When the water was gone, she left the child under a shrub and went off, fifty yards or so. She said, "I can't watch my son die." As she sat, she broke into sobs.

Meanwhile, God heard the boy crying. The angel of God called from Heaven to Hagar, "What's wrong, Hagar? Don't be afraid. God has heard the boy and knows the fix he's in. Up now; go get the boy. Hold him tight. I'm going to make of him a great nation."

Just then God opened her eyes. She looked. She saw a well of water. She went to it and filled her canteen and gave the boy a long, cool drink.

God was on the boy's side as he grew up. He lived out in the desert and became a skilled archer. He lived in the Paran wilderness. And his mother got him a wife from Egypt. (GENESIS 21:9–21 THE MESSAGE)

This is the family tree of Ishmael son of Abraham, the son that Hagar the Egyptian, Sarah's maid, bore to Abraham.

These are the names of Ishmael's sons in the order of their births: Nebaioth, Ishmael's firstborn, Kedar, Adbeel, Mibsam, Mishma, Dumah, Massa, Hadad, Tema, Jetur, Naphish, and Kedemah—all the sons of Ishmael. Their settlements and encampments were named after them. Twelve princes with their twelve tribes.

Ishmael lived 137 years. When he breathed his last and died he was buried with his family. His children settled down all the way from Havilah near Egypt eastward to Shur in the direction of Assyria. The Ishmaelites didn't get along with any of their kin. (GENESIS 25:12–18 THE MESSAGE)

Little did Hagar, Sarah, and Abraham know how Ishmael's birth would affect the world—even today.

And he blessed Joseph and said, "The God before whom my fathers Abraham and Isaac walked, the God who has been my shepherd all my life long to this day, the angel who has redeemed me from all evil, bless the boys; and in them let my name be carried on, and the name of my fathers Abraham and Isaac; and let them grow into a multitude in the midst of the earth" (GENESIS 48:15–16 ESV).

Neither Abraham nor Isaac were perfect men or fathers, but Jacob, their grandson and son respectively, remembered them as men who left behind a heritage of walking before God.

Then Pharaoh commanded all his people, "Every son that is born to the Hebrews you shall cast into the Nile, but you shall let every daughter live." Now a man from the house of Levi went and took as his wife a Levite woman. The woman conceived and bore a son, and when she saw that he was a fine child, she hid him three months. When she could hide him no longer, she took for him a basket made of bulrushes and daubed it with bitumen and pitch. She put the child in it and placed it among the reeds by the river bank. (EXODUS 1:22–2:3 ESV)

The mother of Moses disobeyed a direct command of Pharaoh and risked her own life to save that of her son. God rewarded her risk by using her son to lead his people from the slavery in Egypt that Moses' parents endured.

No carved gods of any size, shape, or form of anything whatever, whether of things that fly or walk or swim. Don't bow down to them and don't serve them because I am GOD, your God, and I'm a most jealous God, punishing the children for any sins their parents pass on to them to the third, and yes, even to the fourth generation of those who hate me. But I'm unswervingly loyal to the thousands who love me and keep my commandments. (EXODUS 20:4–6 THE MESSAGE)

The second of the Ten Commandments concerns God's command that he alone is to be worshiped. Worship of false gods was so serious that those who practiced such idolatry could plunge future generations into sin.

"For this child I prayed, and the LORD has granted me my petition which I asked of Him. Therefore I also have lent him to the LORD; as long as he lives he shall be lent to the LORD." So they worshiped the LORD there. (1 SAMUEL 1:27–28 NKJV)

Hannah, the mother of Samuel, was a godly woman who had her prayers for a child answered through her son Samuel. True to the promise that she made to God, the child Samuel was dedicated to God from his birth and served God all his life.

The LORD said to Samuel, "Behold, I am about to do a thing in Israel at which both ears of everyone who hears it will tingle. In that day I will carry out against Eli all that I have spoken concerning his house, from beginning to end. For I have told him that I am about to judge his house forever for the iniquity which he knew, because his sons brought a curse on themselves and he did not rebuke them. Therefore I have sworn to the house of Eli that the iniquity of Eli's house shall not be atoned for by sacrifice or offering forever" (1 SAMUEL 3:11–14 NASB).

Repeatedly in the Old Testament we see children who are lacking in discipline because their parents, and specifically their fathers, neglected their responsibilities in that area. The household of Eli suffered permanent discipline from God because Eli knew of his sons' wickedness and refused to intervene.

When Samuel grew old, he appointed his sons as Israel's leaders. The name of his firstborn was Joel and the name of his second was Abijah, and they served at Beersheba. But his sons did not follow his ways. They turned aside after dishonest gain and accepted bribes and perverted justice. So all the elders of Israel gathered together and came to Samuel at Ramah. They said to him, "You are old, and your sons do not follow your ways; now appoint a king to lead us, such as all the other nations have" (1 SAMUEL 8:1–5 NIV).

Samuel as related to parenting was an interesting figure in the Old Testament. He was a godly man who had a godly mother, but somewhere along the way the message did not transfer to his own sons. Despite the fact that Samuel had seen Eli's wicked sons and God's punishment of them, he made the same mistakes with his own sons.

After Nathan had gone home, the LORD struck the child that Uriah's wife had borne to David, and he became ill. David pleaded with God for the child. He fasted and spent the nights lying in sackcloth on the ground. The elders of his household stood beside him to get him up from the ground, but he refused, and he would not eat any food with them. On the seventh day the child died. (2 SAMUEL 12:15–18 NIV)

This child that was the product of King David and Bathsheba's adulterous affair died as a consequence of the sin of King David. Even though God had declared that the child would die, David continued to fast and pray for him.

The LORD said to Samuel, "How long will you mourn for Saul, since I have rejected him as king over Israel? Fill your horn with oil and be on your way; I am sending you to Jesse of Bethlehem. I have chosen one of his sons to be king. . . . Invite Jesse to the sacrifice, and I will show you what to do. You are to anoint for me the one I indicate."

When they arrived, Samuel saw Eliab and thought, "Surely the LORD's anointed stands here before the LORD."

But the LORD said to Samuel, "Do not consider his appearance or his height, for I have rejected him. The LORD does not look at the things people look at. People look at the outward appearance, but the LORD looks at the heart."

Then Jesse called Abinadab and had him pass in front of Samuel. But Samuel said, "The LORD has not chosen this one either." Jesse then had Shammah pass by, but Samuel said, "Nor has the LORD chosen this one." Jesse had seven of his sons pass before Samuel, but Samuel said to him, "The LORD has not chosen these." So he asked Jesse, "Are these all the sons you have?"

"There is still the youngest," Jesse answered. "He is tending the sheep."

Samuel said, "Send for him; we will not sit down until he arrives."

So he sent for him and had him brought in. He was glowing with health and had a fine appearance and handsome features.

Then the LORD said, "Rise and anoint him; this is the one." So Samuel took the horn of oil and anointed him in the presence of his brothers, and from that day on the Spirit of the LORD came powerfully upon David. (1 SAMUEL 16:1, 3, 6-13 NIV)

At this time Adonijah, whose mother was Haggith, puffed himself up saying, "I'm the next king!" He made quite a splash, with chariots and riders and fifty men to run ahead of him. His father had spoiled him rotten as a child, never once reprimanding him. Besides that, he was very good-looking and the next in line after Absalom. (1 KINGS 1:5-6 THE MESSAGE)

King David was a mighty warrior and poet, and in many ways lived a life worth imitation. However, as a father, David did not discipline his children. As a result, his two oldest sons, Absalom and Adonijah, both tried to steal the kingdom from him. Parents who do not discipline their children will share in their children's pain.

As for you, my son Solomon, know the God of your father, and serve Him with a whole heart and a willing mind; for the LORD searches all hearts, and understands every intent of the thoughts. If you seek Him, He will let you find Him; but if you forsake Him, He will reject you forever. (1 CHRONICLES 28:9 NASB)

Despite King David's shortcomings as a man and a father—and there were many—he was able to urge his son Solomon to follow in his footsteps as a man who loved, trusted, and obeyed God.

O LORD God of Abraham, Isaac, and Israel, our fathers, keep this forever in the intent of the thoughts of the heart of Your people, and fix their heart toward You. And give my son Solomon a loyal heart to keep Your commandments and Your testimonies and Your statutes, to do all these things, and to build the temple for which I have made provision. (1 CHRONICLES 29:18-19 NKJV)

Then the people of Jerusalem made Ahaziah, Jehoram's youngest son, their next king, since the marauding bands who came with the Arabs had killed all the older sons. So Ahaziah son of Jehoram reigned as king of Judah. Ahaziah was twenty-two years old when he became king, and he reigned in Jerusalem one year. His mother was Athaliah, a granddaughter of King Omri. Ahaziah also followed the evil example of King Ahab's family, for his mother encouraged him in doing wrong. He did what was evil in the LORD's sight, just as Ahab's family had done. They even became his advisers after the death of his father, and they led him to ruin. (2 CHRONICLES 22:1-4 NLT)

The ruin and failure of Ahaziah was tied directly to his wicked mother and her foolish and unrighteous advice. Rather than leading him to wisdom and life, her encouragement led him to his destruction.

Manasseh was twelve years old when he became king, and he reigned fifty-five years in Jerusalem. He did evil in the sight of the LORD according to the abominations of the nations whom the LORD dispossessed before the sons of Israel. For he rebuilt the high places which Hezekiah his father had broken down; he also erected altars for the Baals and made Asherim, and worshiped all the host of heaven and served them. He built altars in the house of the LORD of which the LORD had said, "My name shall be in Jerusalem forever." For he built altars for all the host of heaven in the two courts of the house of the LORD. He made his sons pass through the fire in the valley of Ben-hinnom; and he practiced witchcraft, used divination, practiced sorcery and dealt with mediums and spiritists. He did much evil in the sight of the LORD, provoking Him to anger. **(2 CHRONICLES 33:1–6 NASB)**

Of all of the wicked kings of Judah, Manasseh may have been the most despicable. Though scholars are by no means unanimous, the phrase "He made his sons pass through the fire" can and most likely means that he offered his own sons as human sacrifices. It is little wonder, then, that his reign provoked God to anger.

His sons used to go and hold a feast in the house of each one on his day, and they would send and invite their three sisters to eat and drink with them. When the days of feasting had completed their cycle, Job would send and consecrate them, rising up early in the morning and offering burnt offerings according to the number of them all; for Job said, "Perhaps my sons have sinned and cursed God in their hearts." Thus Job did continually. **(JOB 1:4–5 NASB)**

> *In the days of Job, probably during the days of Abraham, it was customary for the father to act as the priest for his family. Job was exceptional in this role, believing that his influence and prayers for his children could and should even counteract their innermost thoughts and desires.*

Hallelujah! Blessed man, blessed woman, who fear God, who cherish and relish his commandments, their children robust on the earth, and the homes of the upright—how blessed! **(PSALMS 112:1–2 THE MESSAGE)**

> *Parents who know, fear, and serve God will bless future generations just by having been their ancestors.*

Though hand join in hand, the wicked shall not be unpunished: but the seed of the righteous shall be delivered. **(PROVERBS 11:21 KJV)**

> *The expression "hand to hand" was a phrase used in the days of Solomon to refer to the clasping of hands by two people to seal an arrangement, similar to how shaking hands is viewed in American culture. Like a deal that has been finalized, it is sure that those who are wicked will be punished, and that those who are righteous, along with their family, will not be punished.*

These are the words of King Lemuel, the message his mother taught him. **(PROVERBS 31:1 NCV)**

Often we think of fathers teaching sons and mothers teaching daughters, but in the Scriptures we see that both parents have much to teach both children. In Proverbs 31, King Lemuel's mother teaches him what to look for in a wife.

She opens her mouth with wisdom, and the teaching of kindness is on her tongue. She looks well to the ways of her household and does not eat the bread of idleness. Her children rise up and call her blessed; her husband also, and he praises her. **(PROVERBS 31:26–28 ESV)**

Proverbs 31 is a passage taught to the king by his own mother. This passage describes the character and endeavors of a noble woman. This woman was committed to providing for her family, and as a result even her own children blessed her.

God's answer: "Because they abandoned my plain teaching. They wouldn't listen to anything I said, refused to live the way I told them to. Instead they lived any way they wanted and took up with the Baal gods, who they thought would give them what they wanted—following the example of their parents" **(JEREMIAH 9:13–14 THE MESSAGE)**.

The children of Israel did not simply "fall" into sin, nor were they deceived by trickery. Generation after generation intentionally lived contrary to God's Word because they were pursuing their own desires and were doing what they were taught to do by their parents.

Our fathers sinned and are no more, and we have borne their iniquities. **(LAMENTATIONS 5:7 AMP)**

I said to their children in the wilderness, "Do not walk in the statutes of your fathers or keep their ordinances or defile yourselves with their idols. I am the LORD your God; walk in My statutes and keep My ordinances and observe them" (EZEKIEL 20:18–19).

I thank God whom I serve, as did my ancestors, with a clear conscience, as I remember you constantly in my prayers night and day. As I remember your tears, I long to see you, that I may be filled with joy. I am reminded of your sincere faith, a faith that dwelt first in your grandmother Lois and your mother Eunice and now, I am sure, dwells in you as well. (2 TIMOTHY 1:3–5 ESV)

The apostle Paul looked on Timothy as his son in the Christian faith, but Paul also recognized that Timothy's faith had been handed down to him by both his grandmother and his mother.

[With eyes of] faith Isaac, looking far into the future, invoked blessings upon Jacob and Esau. [Prompted] by faith Jacob, when he was dying, blessed each of Joseph's sons and bowed in prayer over the top of his staff. (HEBREWS 11:20–21 AMP)

There may have been no more dysfunctional family than that of the patriarchs Abraham, Isaac, and Jacob. Yet despite their weaknesses, they focused on passing down their faith to their sons.

For you know that it was not with perishable things such as silver or gold that you were redeemed from the empty way of life handed down to you from your ancestors, but with the

precious blood of Christ, a lamb without blemish or defect.
(**1 PETER 1:18–19** NIV)

*The believer in Jesus Christ has the ultimate parental example in
God the Father. Even the best human parents hand down to their
children a legacy and a heritage that is imperfect and short-lived.*

But a portentous day arrived when Herod threw a birthday
party, inviting all the brass and bluebloods in Galilee. Herodias's daughter entered the banquet hall and danced for the
guests. She dazzled Herod and the guests. The king said to
the girl, "Ask me anything. I'll give you anything you want."
Carried away, he kept on, "I swear, I'll split my kingdom with
you if you say so!" She went back to her mother and said,
"What should I ask for?"

"Ask for the head of John the Baptizer" (**MARK 6:21-24 THE
MESSAGE**).

*Any time parenting or family is mentioned in relation to anyone
in the Bible referred to as Herod, rest assured it is a cautionary
tale. Herodias left her first husband, her half uncle, for the Herod
mentioned in Mark 6, also her half uncle. Here, the bounds of
her wickedness know no bounds as she uses her daughter to
extract revenge on John the Baptist for his condemnation of her
wickedness. An unrighteous parent will always attempt to drag
their children down with them.*

3

What God Expects From Children

~~~

And here's the whole challenge of being a parent. Even though your kids will consistently do the exact opposite of what you tell them to do, you have to keep loving them just as much.[5]

Bill Cosby

Many a child has been crushed under the weight of extreme expectations. Whether they are the expectations of parents, grandparents, teachers, or mentors, the expectation itself can at times be more than a child can handle. Some adults live vicariously through children and demand impeccable performance that even they could not live up to. Those are adults whose expectations can and will crush a child's spirit.

For anyone, attempting to meet everyone's expectations can be daunting. This is why it is so important for a child to focus primarily on aligning him or herself with God's expectations. God, as their creator, has expectations for children that often differ from ours. The Almighty is not so much concerned with straight A's, athletic achievement, or scholarships, but rather with the character and integrity of children. Even the holiest of parents can struggle to keep their expectations in balance; those of the heavenly Father, however, are always the best.

Honor your father and your mother, that your days may be long upon the land which the LORD your God is giving you. **(EXODUS 20:12 NKJV)**

> *This verse is so foundational to what the Bible has to say about God's expectations for children that it is quoted in the New Testament several times. (See Deuteronomy 5:16; Matthew 15:4; Matthew 19:19; Mark 7:10; and Luke 18:20.)*

Whoever strikes his father or his mother shall be put to death. Whoever steals a man and sells him, and anyone found in possession of him, shall be put to death. Whoever curses his father or his mother shall be put to death. **(EXODUS 21:15–17 ESV)**

And the LORD spoke to Moses, saying, "Speak to all the congregation of the people of Israel and say to them, You shall be holy, for I the LORD your God am holy. Every one of you shall revere his mother and his father, and you shall keep my Sabbaths: I am the LORD your God" **(LEVITICUS 19:1–3 ESV)**.

> *In the mind of God, reverence for one's parents is just as important as the worship of God and keeping his commandments.*

You shall rise up before the grayheaded and honor the aged, and you shall revere your God; I am the LORD. (LEVITICUS 19:32 NASB)

When a man has a stubborn son, a real rebel who won't do a thing his mother and father tell him, and even though they discipline him he still won't obey, his father and mother shall forcibly bring him before the leaders at the city gate and say to the city fathers, "This son of ours is a stubborn rebel; he won't listen to a thing we say. He's a glutton and a drunk." Then all the men of the town are to throw rocks at him until he's dead. You will have purged the evil pollution from among you. All Israel will hear what's happened and be in awe. (DEUTERONOMY 21:18–21 THE MESSAGE)

So Moses wrote this law and gave it to the priests, the sons of Levi who carried the ark of the covenant of the LORD, and to all the elders of Israel. Then Moses commanded them, saying, "At the end of every seven years, at the time of the year of remission of debts, at the Feast of Booths, when all Israel comes to appear before the LORD your God at the place which He will choose, you shall read this law in front of all Israel in their hearing. Assemble the people, the men and the women and children and the alien who is in your town, so that they may hear and learn and fear the LORD your God, and be careful to observe all the words of this law. Their children, who have not known, will hear and learn to fear the LORD your God, as long as you live on the land which you are about to cross the Jordan to possess" (DEUTERONOMY 31:9–13 NASB).

Robust men and women in their prime, and yes, graybeards and little children. Let them praise the name of GOD—it's the only Name worth praising. His radiance exceeds anything in earth and sky; he's built a monument—his very own people! **(PSALM 148:12–13 THE MESSAGE)**

Listen, my son, to your father's instruction and do not forsake your mother's teaching. They are a garland to grace your head and a chain to adorn your neck. **(PROVERBS 1:8–9 NIV)**

Careful attention paid to parental instruction will bring a child honor; ignoring it will bring dishonor.

My son, do not forget my teaching, but keep my commands in your heart, for they will prolong your life many years and bring you peace and prosperity. Let love and faithfulness never leave you; bind them around your neck, write them on the tablet of your heart. Then you will win favor and a good name in the sight of God and man. **(PROVERBS 3:1–4 NIV)**

My son, obey your father's commands, and don't neglect your mother's instruction. Keep their words always in your heart. Tie them around your neck. When you walk, their counsel will lead you. When you sleep, they will protect you. When you wake up, they will advise you. **(PROVERBS 6:20–22 NLT)**

Children with good sense accept correction from their parents, but stubborn children ignore it completely. **(PROVERBS 13:1 CEV)**

A fool despises his father's instruction and correction, but he who regards reproof acquires prudence. (PROVERBS 15:5 AMP)

A wise son maketh a glad father: but a foolish man despiseth his mother. (PROVERBS 15:20 KJV)

Folly is bound up in the heart of a child, but the rod of discipline drives it far from him. (PROVERBS 22:15 ESV)

Left to themselves, children will stray. Foolishness and folly are deep within the heart of a child, leaving parents with an incredible responsibility to discipline them and separate them from their natural tendency toward folly.

My son, [reverently] fear the LORD and the king, and do not associate with those who are given to change [of allegiance, and are revolutionary], for their calamity shall rise suddenly, and who knows the punishment and ruin which both [the LORD and the king] will bring upon [the rebellious]? (PROVERBS 24:21–22 AMP)

Those with whom a child associates will determine his or her future.

There are those who curse their fathers and do not bless their mothers. There are those who are clean in their own eyes but are not washed of their filth. There are those—how lofty are their eyes, how high their eyelids lift! There are those whose teeth are swords, whose fangs are knives, to devour the poor from off the earth, the needy from among mankind. The leech has two daughters: Give and Give. Three things are never satisfied; four never say, "Enough": Sheol, the barren womb, the land never satisfied with water, and the fire that never says, "Enough." The eye that mocks a father and scorns to obey a mother will be picked out by the ravens of the valley and eaten by the vultures. **(PROVERBS 30:11–17 ESV)**

Don't let the excitement of youth cause you to forget your Creator. Honor him in your youth before you grow old and say, "Life is not pleasant anymore." Remember him before the light of the sun, moon, and stars is dim to your old eyes, and rain clouds continually darken your sky. Remember him before your legs—the guards of your house—start to tremble; and before your shoulders—the strong men—stoop. Remember him before your teeth—your few remaining servants—stop grinding; and before your eyes—the women looking through the windows—see dimly.

Remember him before the door to life's opportunities is closed and the sound of work fades. Now you rise at the first chirping of the birds, but then all their sounds will grow faint.

Remember him before you become fearful of falling and worry about danger in the streets; before your hair turns white like an almond tree in bloom, and you drag along without energy like a dying grasshopper, and the caperberry no longer inspires sexual desire. Remember him before you near the grave, your everlasting home, when the mourners will weep at your funeral.

Yes, remember your Creator now while you are young, before the silver cord of life snaps and the golden bowl is broken. Don't wait until the water jar is smashed at the spring and the pulley is broken at the well. For then the dust will return

to the earth, and the spirit will return to God who gave it.
(ECCLESIASTES 12:1–7 NLT)

> *If some patterns and habits are not established in youth, there
> can come a day when it is too late. Giving God his proper place
> in our lives is one of those habits.*

Now when the Pharisees gathered to him, with some of the
scribes who had come from Jerusalem, they saw that some
of his disciples ate with hands that were defiled, that is, un-
washed. (For the Pharisees and all the Jews do not eat unless
they wash their hands, holding to the tradition of the elders,
and when they come from the marketplace, they do not eat
unless they wash. And there are many other traditions that
they observe, such as the washing of cups and pots and copper
vessels and dining couches.) And the Pharisees and the scribes
asked him, "Why do your disciples not walk according to the
tradition of the elders, but eat with defiled hands?" And he
said to them, "Well did Isaiah prophesy of you hypocrites,
as it is written,

> 'This people honors me with their lips,
> but their heart is far from me;
> in vain do they worship me,
> teaching as doctrines the commandments of men.'

You leave the commandment of God and hold to the tradition of men."

And he said to them, "You have a fine way of rejecting the
commandment of God in order to establish your tradition!
For Moses said, 'Honor your father and your mother'; and,
'Whoever reviles father or mother must surely die.' But you

say, 'If a man tells his father or his mother, "Whatever you would have gained from me is Corban"' (that is, given to God)—then you no longer permit him to do anything for his father or mother, thus making void the word of God by your tradition that you have handed down. And many such things you do" (MARK 7:1–13 ESV).

The Pharisees had declared their money dedicated to God, not to honor God, but as a way of circumventing their God-given responsibilities to take care of their aged parents.

Children, obey your parents in the Lord, for this is right. "Honor your father and mother"—which is the first commandment with a promise—"so that it may be well with you, and that you may live long on the earth" (EPHESIANS 6:1–3 NIV).

This verse gives the principle that obedience will bring self-discipline, and that self-discipline brings stability, which would lead to a long life.

Children, obey your parents in all things, for this is well pleasing to the LORD. (COLOSSIANS 3:20 NKJV)

But if any widow has children or grandchildren, let them first learn to show piety at home and to repay their parents; for this is good and acceptable before God. (1 TIMOTHY 5:4 NKJV)

Do you see what this means—all these pioneers who blazed the way, all these veterans cheering us on? It means we'd better get on with it. Strip down, start running—and never quit! No extra spiritual fat, no parasitic sins. Keep your eyes on Jesus, who both began and finished this race we're in. Study how he did it. Because he never lost sight of where he was headed—that exhilarating finish in and with God—he could put up with anything along the way: Cross, shame, whatever. And now he's there, in the place of honor, right alongside God. When you find yourselves flagging in your faith, go over that story again, item by item, that long litany of hostility he plowed through. That will shoot adrenaline into your souls!

In this all-out match against sin, others have suffered far worse than you, to say nothing of what Jesus went through—all that bloodshed! So don't feel sorry for yourselves. Or have you forgotten how good parents treat children, and that God regards you as his children?

My dear child, don't shrug off God's discipline, but don't be crushed by it either. It's the child he loves that he disciplines; the child he embraces, he also corrects. God is educating you; that's why you must never drop out. He's treating you as dear children. This trouble you're in isn't punishment; it's training, the normal experience of children. Only irresponsible parents leave children to fend for themselves. Would you prefer an irresponsible God? We respect our own parents for training and not spoiling us, so why not embrace God's training so we can truly live? While we were children, our parents did what seemed best to them. But God is doing what is best for us, training us to live God's holy best. At the time, discipline isn't much fun. It always feels like it's going against the grain. Later, of course, it pays off handsomely, for it's the well-trained who find themselves mature in their relationship with God. (HEBREWS 12:1–11 THE MESSAGE)

Children have a responsibility to cooperate with the discipline that is handed out by both their heavenly Father and earthly parents.

Likewise, you who are younger and of lesser rank, be subject to the elders (the ministers and spiritual guides of the church)—[giving them due respect and yielding to their counsel]. Clothe (apron) yourselves, all of you, with humility [as the garb of a servant, so that its covering cannot possibly be stripped from you, with freedom from pride and arrogance] toward one another. For God sets Himself against the proud (the insolent, the overbearing, the disdainful, the presumptuous, the boastful)—[and He opposes, frustrates, and defeats them], but gives grace (favor, blessing) to the humble. (1 PETER 5:5 AMP)

4

How Children's Behavior Affects Their Parents ... and Their Own Future

———

I understand more and more how true Daddy's words were when he said: all children must look after their own upbringing. Parents can only give good advice or put them on the right paths, but the final forming of a person's character lies in their own hands.[6]

Anne Frank

For obvious reasons, children are almost always associated with the future. We think of children as having their whole life in front of them, and we tell them that they can be anything they want to be. Often we are so focused on growing and developing who children will become that we can forget who and what they are.

Children, certainly in their formative years, are already more than capable of amazing things. Mozart, for example, was proficient in the piano and violin—even writing entire symphonies—by the time he was ten years old. Chess prodigy Bobby Fischer won the Chess Championship of the United States and achieved the title of Grandmaster, all before he was old enough to drive a car.

Most children will not be prodigies in the same way that Mozart or Bobby Fischer were, but every child's actions will leave a mark on the world around them. Children, though they have much maturing and growing to do, will have a positive or negative impact on their parents, siblings, and everyone else with whom they come into contact.

Even at an early age, righteousness matters!

Adam made love to his wife Eve, and she became pregnant and gave birth to Cain. She said, "With the help of the LORD I have brought forth a man." Later she gave birth to his brother Abel.

Now Abel kept flocks, and Cain worked the soil. In the course of time Cain brought some of the fruits of the soil as an offering to the LORD. And Abel also brought an offering—fat portions from some of the firstborn of his flock. The LORD looked with favor on Abel and his offering, but on Cain and his offering he did not look with favor. So Cain was very angry, and his face was downcast.

Then the LORD said to Cain, "Why are you angry? Why is your face downcast? If you do what is right, will you not be accepted? But if you do not do what is right, sin is crouching at your door; it desires to have you, but you must rule over it."

Now Cain said to his brother Abel, "Let's go out to the field." While they were in the field, Cain attacked his brother Abel and killed him.

Then the LORD said to Cain, "Where is your brother Abel?"

"I don't know," he replied. "Am I my brother's keeper?"

The LORD said, "What have you done? Listen! Your brother's blood cries out to me from the ground. Now you are under a curse and driven from the ground, which opened its mouth to receive your brother's blood from your hand. When you work the ground, it will no longer yield its crops for you. You will be a restless wanderer on the earth."

Cain said to the LORD, "My punishment is more than I can bear. Today you are driving me from the land, and I will be hidden from your presence; I will be a restless wanderer on the earth, and whoever finds me will kill me."

But the LORD said to him, "Not so; anyone who kills Cain will suffer vengeance seven times over." Then the LORD put a mark on Cain so that no one who found him would kill him. So Cain went out from the LORD's presence and lived in the land of Nod, east of Eden. (GENESIS 4:1-16 NIV)

So remember this and keep it firmly in mind: The LORD is God both in heaven and on earth, and there is no other. If you obey all the decrees and commands I am giving you today, all will be well with you and your children. I am giving you these instructions so you will enjoy a long life in the land the LORD your God is giving you for all time. (DEUTERONOMY 4:39–40 NLT)

"Cursed is he who dishonors his father or mother." And all the people shall say, "Amen" (DEUTERONOMY 27:16 NASB).

Elimelech died and Naomi was left, she and her two sons. The sons took Moabite wives; the name of the first was Orpah, the second Ruth. They lived there in Moab for the next ten years. But then the two brothers, Mahlon and Kilion, died. Now the woman was left without either her young men or her husband.

One day she got herself together, she and her two daughters-in-law, to leave the country of Moab and set out for home; she had heard that God had been pleased to visit his people and give them food. And so she started out from the place she had been living, she and her two daughters-in-law with her, on the road back to the land of Judah.

After a short while on the road, Naomi told her two daughters-in-law, "Go back. Go home and live with your mothers. And may God treat you as graciously as you treated your deceased husbands and me. May God give each of you a new home and a new husband!" She kissed them and they cried openly.

They said, "No, we're going on with you to your people."

But Naomi was firm: "Go back, my dear daughters. Why would you come with me? Do you suppose I still have sons in my womb who can become your future husbands? Go back, dear daughters—on your way, please! I'm too old to get a husband. Why, even if I said, 'There's still hope!' and this very night got a man and had sons, can you imagine being satisfied to wait until they were grown? Would you wait that long to get married again? No, dear daughters; this is a bitter pill for me to swallow—more bitter for me than for you. God has dealt me a hard blow."

Again they cried openly. Orpah kissed her mother-in-law good-bye; but Ruth embraced her and held on. Naomi said, "Look, your sister-in-law is going back home to live with her own people and gods; go with her."

But Ruth said, "Don't force me to leave you; don't make me go home. Where you go, I go; and where you live, I'll live. Your people are my people, your God is my god; where you die, I'll die, and that's where I'll be buried, so help me God—not even death itself is going to come between us!"

When Naomi saw that Ruth had her heart set on going with her, she gave in. And so the two of them traveled on together to Bethlehem. (RUTH 1:3–19 THE MESSAGE)

Decisions of adult children—even in-laws—affect families. For the rest of Naomi's and Ruth's story, read the book of Ruth.

Eli's own sons were a bad lot. They didn't know GOD and could not have cared less about the customs of priests among the people. Ordinarily, when someone offered a sacrifice, the priest's servant was supposed to come up and, while the meat was boiling, stab a three-pronged fork into the cooking pot. The priest then got whatever came up on the fork. But this is how Eli's sons treated all the Israelites who came to Shiloh to offer sacrifices to GOD. Before they had even burned the fat to GOD, the priest's servant would interrupt whoever was sacrificing and say, "Hand over some of that meat for the priest to roast. He doesn't like boiled meat; he likes his rare." If the man objected, "First let the fat be burned—God's portion!—then take all you want," the servant would demand, "No, I want it now. If you won't give it, I'll take it." It was a horrible sin these young servants were committing—and right in the presence of GOD!—desecrating the holy offerings to GOD.

In the midst of all this, Samuel, a boy dressed in a priestly linen tunic, served GOD. Additionally, every year his mother would make him a little robe cut to his size and bring it to him when she and her husband came for the annual sacrifice. Eli would bless Elkanah and his wife, saying, "GOD give you children to replace this child you have dedicated to GOD." Then they would go home.

GOD was most especially kind to Hannah. She had three more sons and two daughters! The boy Samuel stayed at the sanctuary and grew up with GOD.

By this time Eli was very old. He kept getting reports on how his sons were ripping off the people and sleeping with the women who helped out at the sanctuary. Eli took them to task: "What's going on here? Why are you doing these things? I hear story after story of your corrupt and evil carrying on. Oh, my sons, this is not right! These are terrible reports I'm getting, stories spreading right and left among GOD's people! If you sin against another person, there's help—God's help. But if you sin against GOD, who is around to help?"

But they were far gone in disobedience and refused to listen to a thing their father said. So GOD, who was fed up with them, decreed their death. But the boy Samuel was very much alive, growing up, blessed by GOD and popular with the people.

A holy man came to Eli and said: "This is God's message: I revealed myself openly to your ancestors when they were Pharaoh's slaves in Egypt. Out of all the tribes of Israel, I chose your family to be my priests: to preside at the Altar, to burn incense, to wear the priestly robes in my presence. I put your ancestral family in charge of all the sacrificial offerings of Israel. So why do you now treat as mere loot these very sacrificial offerings that I commanded for my worship? Why do you treat your sons better than me, turning them loose to get fat on these offerings, and ignoring me? Therefore—this is God's word, the God of Israel speaking—I once said that you and your ancestral family would be my priests indefinitely, but now—God's word, remember!—there is no way this can continue. I honor those who honor me; those who scorn me I demean. Be well warned: It won't be long before I wipe out both your family and your future family. No one in your family will make it to old age! You'll see good things that I'm doing in Israel, but you'll see it and weep, for no one in your family will live to enjoy it. I will leave one person to serve at my Altar, but it will be a hard life, with many tears. Everyone else in your family will die before their time. What happens to your two sons, Hophni and Phinehas, will be the proof: Both will die the same day. Then I'll establish for myself a true priest. He'll do what I want him to do, be what I want him to be. I'll make his position secure and he'll do his work freely in the service of my anointed one. Survivors from your family will come to him begging for handouts, saying, 'Please, give me some priest work, just enough to put some food on the table'" (1 SAMUEL 2:12–36 THE MESSAGE).

The contrast between Samuel and the sons of Eli could not have been more severe. The impact of their lives showed just how different they were.

Then the men of the city said to Elisha, "Please notice, the situation of this city is pleasant, as my lord sees; but the water is bad, and the ground barren."

And he said, "Bring me a new bowl, and put salt in it." So they brought it to him. Then he went out to the source of the water, and cast in the salt there, and said, "Thus says the LORD: 'I have healed this water; from it there shall be no more death or barrenness.'" So the water remains healed to this day, according to the word of Elisha which he spoke.

Then he went up from there to Bethel; and as he was going up the road, some youths came from the city and mocked him, and said to him, "Go up, you baldhead! Go up, you baldhead!"

So he turned around and looked at them, and pronounced a curse on them in the name of the LORD. And two female bears came out of the woods and mauled forty-two of the youths.

Then he went from there to Mount Carmel, and from there he returned to Samaria. (2 KINGS 2:19–25 NKJV)

Imagine if this judgment were enacted today—children might reconsider disrespecting their elders.

LORD, our Lord, how majestic is your name in all the earth! You have set your glory in the heavens. Through the praise of children and infants you have established a stronghold against your enemies, to silence the foe and the avenger. **(PSALM 8:1–2 NIV)**

Unless the LORD builds a house, the work of the builders is wasted. Unless the LORD protects a city, guarding it with sentries will do no good. It is useless for you to work so hard from early morning until late at night, anxiously working for food to eat; for God gives rest to his loved ones. Children are a gift from the LORD; they are a reward from him. Children born to a young man are like arrows in a warrior's hands. How joyful is the man whose quiver is full of them! He will not be put to shame when he confronts his accusers at the city gates. **(PSALM 127:1–5 NLT)**

I saw among the simple, I noticed among the young men, a youth who had no sense. **(PROVERBS 7:7 NIV)**

Even though children must grow and mature, they will still need to operate with wisdom and common sense.

Wise son, glad father; stupid son, sad mother. **(PROVERBS 10:1 THE MESSAGE)**

King Solomon had a way of relating wisdom that was succinct and to the point. This verse is a prime example.

A self-confident and foolish son is a grief to his father and bitterness to her who bore him. **(PROVERBS 17:25 AMP)**

Children who mistreat their father or chase away their mother are an embarrassment and a public disgrace. If you stop listening to instruction, my child, you will turn your back on knowledge. **(PROVERBS 19:26–27 NLT)**

It makes good sense to obey the Law of God, but you disgrace your parents if you make friends with worthless nobodies. **(PROVERBS 28:7 CEV)**

Correct your son, and he will give you comfort; He will also delight your soul. **(PROVERBS 29:17 NASB)**

5

Sons and Daughters in Particular

By profession, I am a soldier and take pride in that fact. But I am prouder—infinitely prouder—to be a father. A soldier destroys in order to build; the father only builds, never destroys. The one has the potentiality of death; the other embodies creation and life. And while the hordes of death are mighty, the battalions of life are mightier still. It is my hope that my son, when I am gone, will remember me not from the battlefield but in the home repeating with him our simple daily prayer, "Our Father who art in Heaven."[7]

General Douglas MacArthur

I'll never forget the day I told Ronald Reagan that Carolyn was going to have a baby. "Pray for a girl," he said. "What about Ron?" I asked, referring to his son, who was still living at home at the time. "Oh, I love Ron," he said, "but having a little girl is like seeing your wife grow up all over again."[8]

Michael K. Deaver

Sons and daughters are different.

This may seem like an obvious statement, but it is a fact that much of modern culture seems to have forgotten. Much of this struggle is due to a lack of understanding that being different does not imply a comparison. One is not better or worse, but rather their heavenly Father has created them distinct, each with wonderfully unique talents and abilities.

Life in the biblical world was not really all that different. Boys were often valued for their ability to carry on the family name and to provide for the family, particularly the parents as they aged. Girls were treasured for their ability to carry children and to work with their hands. Though there are places in the Scripture that focus on the differences between sons and daughters, both sexes are the delight of their heavenly Father.

SONS

Then his brothers went to feed their father's flock in Shechem. And Israel said to Joseph, "Are not your brothers feeding the flock in Shechem? Come, I will send you to them." So he said to him, "Here I am." Then he said to him, "Please go and see if it is well with your brothers and well with the flocks, and bring back word to me." So he sent him out of the Valley of Hebron, and he went to Shechem.

Now a certain man found him, and there he was, wandering in the field. And the man asked him, saying, "What are you seeking?"

So he said, "I am seeking my brothers. Please tell me where they are feeding their flocks."

And the man said, "They have departed from here, for I heard them say, 'Let us go to Dothan.'" So Joseph went after his brothers and found them in Dothan.

Now when they saw him afar off, even before he came near them, they conspired against him to kill him. Then they said to one another, "Look, this dreamer is coming! Come therefore, let us now kill him and cast him into some pit; and we shall say, 'Some wild beast has devoured him.' We shall see what will become of his dreams!"

But Reuben heard it, and he delivered him out of their hands, and said, "Let us not kill him." And Reuben said to them, "Shed no blood, but cast him into this pit which is in the wilderness, and do not lay a hand on him"—that he might deliver him out of their hands, and bring him back to his father.

So it came to pass, when Joseph had come to his brothers, that they stripped Joseph of his tunic, the tunic of many colors that was on him. Then they took him and cast him into a pit. And the pit was empty; there was no water in it.

And they sat down to eat a meal. Then they lifted their eyes and looked, and there was a company of Ishmaelites, coming from Gilead with their camels, bearing spices, balm, and myrrh, on their way to carry them down to Egypt. So

Judah said to his brothers, "What profit is there if we kill our brother and conceal his blood? Come and let us sell him to the Ishmaelites, and let not our hand be upon him, for he is our brother and our flesh." And his brothers listened. Then Midianite traders passed by; so the brothers pulled Joseph up and lifted him out of the pit, and sold him to the Ishmaelites for twenty shekels of silver. And they took Joseph to Egypt.

Then Reuben returned to the pit, and indeed Joseph was not in the pit; and he tore his clothes. And he returned to his brothers and said, "The lad is no more; and I, where shall I go?"

So they took Joseph's tunic, killed a kid of the goats, and dipped the tunic in the blood. Then they sent the tunic of many colors, and they brought it to their father and said, "We have found this. Do you know whether it is your son's tunic or not?"

And he recognized it and said, "It is my son's tunic. A wild beast has devoured him. Without doubt Joseph is torn to pieces." Then Jacob tore his clothes, put sackcloth on his waist, and mourned for his son many days. And all his sons and all his daughters arose to comfort him; but he refused to be comforted, and he said, "For I shall go down into the grave to my son in mourning." Thus his father wept for him. (GENESIS 37:12–35 NKJV)

There may be no greater example of the best and worst of raising sons than that of Jacob and his brood of children.

Jacob called his sons and said, "Gather around. I want to tell you what you can expect in the days to come."

Come together, listen sons of Jacob, listen to Israel your father.

Reuben, you're my firstborn, my strength, first proof of my manhood, at the top in honor and at the top in power, but like a bucket of water spilled, you'll be at the top no more, because you climbed into your father's marriage bed, mounting that couch, and you defiled it.

Simeon and Levi are two of a kind, ready to fight at the drop of a hat. I don't want anything to do with their vendettas, want no part in their bitter feuds; they kill men in fits of temper, slash oxen on a whim.

A curse on their uncontrolled anger, on their indiscriminate wrath. I'll throw them out with the trash; I'll shred and scatter them like confetti throughout Israel.

You, Judah, your brothers will praise you: your fingers on your enemies' throat, while your brothers honor you. You're a lion's cub, Judah, home fresh from the kill, my son. Look at him, crouched like a lion, king of beasts; who dares mess with him? The scepter shall not leave Judah; he'll keep a firm grip on the command staff until the ultimate ruler comes and the nations obey him. He'll tie up his donkey to the grapevine, his purebred prize to a sturdy branch. He will wash his shirt in wine and his cloak in the blood of grapes, his eyes will be darker than wine, his teeth whiter than milk.

Zebulun settles down on the seashore; he's a safe harbor for ships, right alongside Sidon. Issachar is one tough donkey crouching between the corrals; when he saw how good the place was, how pleasant the country, he gave up his freedom and went to work as a slave.

Dan will handle matters of justice for his people; he will hold his own just fine among the tribes of Israel. Dan is only a small snake in the grass, a lethal serpent in ambush by the road when he strikes a horse in the heel, and brings its huge rider crashing down.

I wait in hope for your salvation, GOD.

Gad will be attacked by bandits, but he will trip them up.

Asher will become famous for rich foods, candies and sweets fit for kings.

Naphtali is a deer running free that gives birth to lovely fawns. Joseph is a wild donkey, a wild donkey by a spring, spirited donkeys on a hill. The archers with malice attacked, shooting their hate-tipped arrows; but he held steady under fire, his bow firm, his arms limber, with the backing of the Champion of Jacob, the Shepherd, the Rock of Israel. The God of your father—may he help you! And may The Strong God—may he give you his blessings, blessings tumbling out of the skies, blessings bursting up from the Earth—blessings of breasts and womb. May the blessings of your father exceed the blessings of the ancient mountains, surpass the delights of the eternal hills; may they rest on the head of Joseph, on the brow of the one consecrated among his brothers.

Benjamin is a ravenous wolf; all morning he gorges on his kill, at evening divides up what's left over.

All these are the tribes of Israel, the twelve tribes. And this is what their father said to them as he blessed them, blessing each one with his own special farewell blessing.

Then he instructed them: "I am about to be gathered to my people. Bury me with my fathers in the cave which is in the field of Ephron the Hittite, the cave in the field of Machpelah facing Mamre in the land of Canaan, the field Abraham bought from Ephron the Hittite for a burial plot. Abraham and his wife Sarah were buried there; Isaac and his wife Rebekah were buried there; I also buried Leah there. The field and the cave were bought from the Hittites."

Jacob finished instructing his sons, pulled his feet into bed, breathed his last, and was gathered to his people. (**GENESIS 49:1–33 THE MESSAGE**)

When the LORD brings you into the land of the Canaanites, as he swore to you and your fathers, and shall give it to you, you shall set apart to the LORD all that first opens the womb. All the firstborn of your animals that are males shall be the LORD's. Every firstborn of a donkey you shall redeem with a lamb, or if you will not redeem it you shall break its neck. Every firstborn of man among your sons you shall redeem. And when in time to come your son asks you, "What does this mean?" you shall say to him, "By a strong hand the LORD brought us out of Egypt, from the house of slavery. For when Pharaoh stubbornly refused to let us go, the LORD killed all the firstborn in the land of Egypt, both the firstborn of man and the firstborn of animals. Therefore I sacrifice to the LORD all the males that first open the womb, but all the firstborn of my sons I redeem." It shall be as a mark on your hand or frontlets between your eyes, for by a strong hand the LORD brought us out of Egypt. (**EXODUS 13:11–16 ESV**)

A man might have two wives, one he loves and one he doesn't. Both wives might have sons by him. If the older son belongs to the wife he does not love, when that man wills his property to his sons he must not give the son of the wife he loves what belongs to the older son, the son of the wife he does not love. He must agree to give the older son two shares of everything he owns, even though the older son is from the wife he does not love. That son was the first to prove his father could have children, so he has the rights that belong to the older son. If someone has a son who is stubborn, who turns against his father and mother and doesn't obey them or listen when they correct him, his parents must take him to the elders at the city gate. They will say to the elders, "Our son is stubborn and turns against us. He will not obey us. He eats too much, and he is always drunk." Then all the men in his town must throw stones at him until he dies. Get rid of the evil among you, because then all the people of Israel will hear about this and be afraid. (DEUTERONOMY 21:15-21 NCV)

A foolish son is destruction to his father, and the contentions of a wife are a constant dripping. House and wealth are an inheritance from fathers, but a prudent wife is from the LORD. (PROVERBS 19:13-14 NASB)

To illustrate the point further, Jesus told them this story: "A man had two sons. The younger son told his father, 'I want my share of your estate now before you die.' So his father agreed to divide his wealth between his sons.

A few days later this younger son packed all his belongings and moved to a distant land, and there he wasted all his money in wild living. About the time his money ran out, a great famine swept over the land, and he began to starve. He persuaded a local farmer to hire him, and the man sent him into his fields to feed the pigs. The young man became so hungry that even the pods he was feeding the pigs looked good to him. But no one gave him anything.

When he finally came to his senses, he said to himself, 'At home even the hired servants have food enough to spare, and here I am dying of hunger! I will go home to my father and say, "Father, I have sinned against both heaven and you, and I am no longer worthy of being called your son. Please take me on as a hired servant."'

So he returned home to his father. And while he was still a long way off, his father saw him coming. Filled with love and compassion, he ran to his son, embraced him, and kissed him. His son said to him, 'Father, I have sinned against both heaven and you, and I am no longer worthy of being called your son.'

But his father said to the servants, 'Quick! Bring the finest robe in the house and put it on him. Get a ring for his finger and sandals for his feet. And kill the calf we have been fattening. We must celebrate with a feast, for this son of mine was dead and has now returned to life. He was lost, but now he is found.' So the party began.

Meanwhile, the older son was in the fields working. When he returned home, he heard music and dancing in the house, and he asked one of the servants what was going on. 'Your brother is back,' he was told, 'and your father has killed the fattened calf. We are celebrating because of his safe return.'

The older brother was angry and wouldn't go in. His father came out and begged him, but he replied, 'All these years I've slaved for you and never once refused to do a single thing you told me to. And in all that time you never gave me even one young goat for a feast with my friends. Yet when this son of yours comes back after squandering your money on prostitutes, you celebrate by killing the fattened calf!'

His father said to him, 'Look, dear son, you have always stayed by me, and everything I have is yours. We had to celebrate this happy day. For your brother was dead and has come back to life! He was lost, but now he is found!'" **(LUKE 15:11–32 NLT)**.

The parable of the prodigal son contains the account of two of the most famous sons and brothers in the entire Scriptures.

DAUGHTERS

Soon after that, the servant loaded ten of Abraham's camels with valuable gifts. Then he set out for the city in northern Syria, where Abraham's brother Nahor lived. When he got there, he let the camels rest near the well outside the city. It was late afternoon, the time when the women came out for water. The servant prayed: You, LORD, are the God my master Abraham worships. Please keep your promise to him and let me find a wife for Isaac today. The young women of the city will soon come to this well for water, and I'll ask one of them for a drink. If she gives me a drink and then offers to get some water for my camels, I'll know she is the one you have chosen and that you have kept your promise to my master. **(GENESIS 24:10–14 CEV)**

The women of the Old Testament were incredibly industrious, particularly when one considers the difficulties associated with living in a society that contained little of today's modern conveniences.

While he was still praying, a beautiful unmarried young woman came by with a water jar on her shoulder. She was Rebekah, the daughter of Bethuel, the son of Abraham's brother Nahor and his wife Milcah. Rebekah walked past Abraham's servant, then went over to the well, and filled her water jar. When she started back, Abraham's servant ran to her and said, "Please let me have a drink of water."

"I'll be glad to," she answered. Then she quickly took the jar from her shoulder and held it while he drank. After he had finished, she said, "Now I'll give your camels all the water they want." She quickly poured out water for them, and she kept going back for more, until his camels had drunk all they wanted. Abraham's servant did not say a word, but he watched everything Rebekah did, because he wanted to know for certain if this was the woman the LORD had chosen. (GENESIS 24:15–21 CEV)

After the servant had determined that Rebekah was the Lord's choice, and he had met with her family, he wanted to be on his way the next day. Rebekah's mother and brother wanted her to stay with them for a week or so, but the servant was insistent.

They answered, "Let's ask Rebekah what she wants to do." They called her and asked, "Are you willing to leave with this man right now?"

"Yes," she answered.

So they agreed to let Rebekah and an old family servant woman leave immediately with Abraham's servant and his men. They gave Rebekah their blessing and said, "We pray that God will give you many children and grandchildren and that he will help them defeat their enemies." Afterwards, Rebekah and the young women who were to travel with her prepared to leave. Then they got on camels and left with Abraham's servant and his men. (GENESIS 24:57–61 CEV)

Now the priest of Midian had seven daughters. And they came and drew water, and they filled the troughs to water their father's flock. Then the shepherds came and drove them away; but Moses stood up and helped them, and watered their flock.

When they came to Reuel their father, he said, "How is it that you have come so soon today?"

And they said, "An Egyptian delivered us from the hand of the shepherds, and he also drew enough water for us and watered the flock."

So he said to his daughters, "And where is he? Why is it that you have left the man? Call him, that he may eat bread."

Then Moses was content to live with the man, and he gave Zipporah his daughter to Moses. And she bore him a son. He called his name Gershom, for he said, "I have been a stranger in a foreign land." Now it happened in the process of time that the king of Egypt died. Then the children of Israel groaned because of the bondage, and they cried out; and their cry came up to God because of the bondage. So God heard their groaning, and God remembered His covenant with Abraham, with Isaac, and with Jacob. And God looked upon the children of Israel, and God acknowledged them. (EXODUS 2:16–25 NKJV)

Then came the daughters of Zelophehad the son of Hepher, the son of Gilead, the son of Machir, the son of Manasseh, from the families of Manasseh the son of Joseph; and these were the names of his daughters: Mahlah, Noah, Hoglah, Milcah, and Tirzah. And they stood before Moses, before

Eleazar the priest, and before the leaders and all the congregation, by the doorway of the tabernacle of meeting, saying: "Our father died in the wilderness; but he was not in the company of those who gathered together against the LORD, in company with Korah, but he died in his own sin; and he had no sons. Why should the name of our father be removed from among his family because he had no son? Give us a possession among our father's brothers."

So Moses brought their case before the LORD. And the LORD spoke to Moses, saying: "The daughters of Zelophehad speak what is right; you shall surely give them a possession of inheritance among their father's brothers, and cause the inheritance of their father to pass to them. And you shall speak to the children of Israel, saying: 'If a man dies and has no son, then you shall cause his inheritance to pass to his daughter. If he has no daughter, then you shall give his inheritance to his brothers. If he has no brothers, then you shall give his inheritance to his father's brothers. And if his father has no brothers, then you shall give his inheritance to the relative closest to him in his family, and he shall possess it.'" And it shall be to the children of Israel a statute of judgment, just as the LORD commanded Moses. **(NUMBERS 27:1–11 NKJV)**

He had also seven sons and three daughters. And he called the name of the first daughter Jemimah, and the name of the second Keziah, and the name of the third Keren-happuch. And in all the land there were no women so beautiful as Job's daughters. And their father gave them an inheritance among their brothers. **(JOB 42:13–15 ESV)**

Hebrew scholars suggest these meanings for the names of Job's daughters: Jemimah *means dove;* Keziah *is another spelling of the word* cassia. *(In the Gospels, when the wise men brought their gifts to the infant Jesus, they brought gifts of cassia, aloes, and myrrh, all of which were fragrances and incenses that were expensive, rare, and beautiful.)* Keren-happuch *literally means the horn of adornment and is a reference to the outward beauty that comes from an inward character.*

6

Children and Miracles

⸻⸺

Instead of wishing away nine months of pregnancy, I'd have cherished every moment, realizing that the wonderment growing inside me was the only chance in life to assist God in a miracle.[9]

Erma Bombeck

If there is one thing that the Bible is full of, it is miracles. Seas divide, people are resurrected from the dead, giants are slain, the earth swallows complainers, fire consumes the wicked, a man rides a chariot of fire, the sick are healed, and donkeys even talk. The Bible is nothing if not a record of the miraculous.

It may come as a surprise, then, to realize just how many of the Bible's miracles are focused on children. At first glance, that might seem surprising. But if you have ever spent any time in a Neonatal Intensive Care Unit, the children's wing of a cancer hospital, or somewhere like the Ronald McDonald house, it makes perfect sense. Even those who have accepted the tension that is God's sovereignty and human suffering struggle when they see a child enduring brutal hardship.

We just sometimes forget that when God looks at all of us, no matter our age, he sees children.

※

Some time later, the LORD spoke to Abram in a vision and said to him, "Do not be afraid, Abram, for I will protect you, and your reward will be great."

But Abram replied, "O Sovereign LORD, what good are all your blessings when I don't even have a son? Since you've given me no children, Eliezer of Damascus, a servant in my household, will inherit all my wealth. You have given me no descendants of my own, so one of my servants will be my heir." Then the LORD said to him, "No, your servant will not be your heir, for you will have a son of your own who will be your heir."

Then the LORD took Abram outside and said to him, "Look up into the sky and count the stars if you can. That's how many descendants you will have!"

And Abram believed the LORD, and the LORD counted him as righteous because of his faith. (GENESIS 15:1-6 NLT)

Often in the Bible God uses children to stretch the faith of their parents.

Then God said to Abraham, "As for Sarai your wife, you shall not call her name Sarai, but Sarah shall be her name. And I will bless her and also give you a son by her; then I will bless her, and she shall be a mother of nations; kings of peoples shall be from her."

Then Abraham fell on his face and laughed, and said in his heart, "Shall a child be born to a man who is one hundred years old? And shall Sarah, who is ninety years old, bear a child?" . . . And He said, "I will certainly return to you according to the time of life, and behold, Sarah your wife shall have a son."

(Sarah was listening in the tent door which was behind him.) Now Abraham and Sarah were old, well advanced in age; and Sarah had passed the age of childbearing. Therefore Sarah laughed within herself, saying, "After I have grown old, shall I have pleasure, my Lord being old also?" And the LORD said to Abraham, "Why did Sarah laugh, saying, 'Shall I surely bear a child, since I am old?'

Is anything too hard for the LORD? At the appointed time I will return to you, according to the time of life, and Sarah shall have a son."

But Sarah denied it, saying, "I did not laugh," for she was afraid.

And He said, "No, but you did laugh!" . . .

And the LORD visited Sarah as He had said, and the LORD did for Sarah as He had spoken. For Sarah conceived and bore Abraham a son in his old age, at the set time of which God had spoken to him. And Abraham called the name of his son who was born to him—whom Sarah bore to him—Isaac. Then Abraham circumcised his son Isaac when he was eight days old, as God had commanded him. Now Abraham was one hundred years old when his son Isaac was born to him. And Sarah said, "God has made me laugh, and all who hear will laugh with me." She also said, "Who would have said to Abraham that Sarah would nurse children? For I have borne him a son in his old age" (GENESIS 17:15–17; 18:10–15; 21:1–7 NKJV).

When Rachel saw that she wasn't having any children for Jacob, she became jealous of her sister. She pleaded with Jacob, "Give me children, or I'll die!"

Then Jacob became furious with Rachel. "Am I God?" he asked. "He's the one who has kept you from having children!"

Then Rachel told him, "Take my maid, Bilhah, and sleep with her. She will bear children for me, and through her I can have a family, too." So Rachel gave her servant, Bilhah, to Jacob as a wife, and he slept with her. Bilhah became pregnant and presented him with a son. Rachel named him Dan, for she said, "God has vindicated me! He has heard my request and given me a son." Then Bilhah became pregnant again and gave Jacob a second son. Rachel named him Naphtali, for she said, "I have struggled hard with my sister, and I'm winning!"

Meanwhile, Leah realized that she wasn't getting pregnant anymore, so she took her servant, Zilpah, and gave her to Jacob as a wife. Soon Zilpah presented him with a son. Leah named him Gad, for she said, "How fortunate I am!" Then Zilpah gave Jacob a second son. And Leah named him Asher, for she said, "What joy is mine! Now the other women will celebrate with me."

One day during the wheat harvest, Reuben found some mandrakes growing in a field and brought them to his mother, Leah. Rachel begged Leah, "Please give me some of your son's mandrakes."

But Leah angrily replied, "Wasn't it enough that you stole my husband? Now will you steal my son's mandrakes, too?"

Rachel answered, "I will let Jacob sleep with you tonight if you give me some of the mandrakes."

So that evening, as Jacob was coming home from the fields, Leah went out to meet him. "You must come and sleep with me tonight!" she said. "I have paid for you with some mandrakes that my son found." So that night he slept with Leah. And God answered Leah's prayers. She became pregnant again and gave birth to a fifth son for Jacob. She named him Issachar, for she said, "God has rewarded me for giving my servant to my husband as a wife." Then Leah became pregnant again and gave birth to a sixth son for Jacob. She named him Zebulun, for she said, "God has given me a good reward. Now my husband will treat me with respect, for I have given him six sons." Later she gave birth to a daughter and named her Dinah.

Then God remembered Rachel's plight and answered her prayers by enabling her to have children. She became pregnant and gave birth to a son. "God has removed my disgrace," she said. And she named him Joseph, for she said, "May the LORD add yet another son to my family" (GENESIS 30:1–24 NLT).

Now a man from the house of Levi went and married a daughter of Levi. The woman conceived and bore a son; and when she saw that he was beautiful, she hid him for three months. But when she could hide him no longer, she got him a wicker basket and covered it over with tar and pitch Then she put the child into it and set it among the reeds by the bank of the Nile. His sister stood at a distance to find out what would happen to him.

The daughter of Pharaoh came down to bathe at the Nile, with her maidens walking alongside the Nile; and she saw the basket among the reeds and sent her maid, and she brought it to her. When she opened it, she saw the child, and behold, the boy was crying. And she had pity on him and said, "This is one of the Hebrews' children." Then his sister said to Pharaoh's daughter, "Shall I go and call a nurse for you from the Hebrew women that she may nurse the child for you?" Pharaoh's daughter said to her, "Go ahead." So the girl went and called the child's mother. Then Pharaoh's daughter said to her, "Take this child away and nurse him for me and I will give you your wages." So the woman took the child and nursed him. The child grew, and she brought him to Pharaoh's daughter and he became her son. And she named him Moses, and said, "Because I drew him out of the water" (EXODUS 2:1–10 NASB).

The birth of Moses was a miracle that exhibited the faith of his parents and would save the nation of Israel from slavery in Egypt.

Elkanah lived in Ramah, a town in the hill country of Ephraim. His great-great-grandfather was Zuph, so Elkanah was a member of the Zuph clan of the Ephraim tribe. Elkanah's father was Jeroham, his grandfather was Elihu, and his great-grandfather was Tohu.

Elkanah had two wives, Hannah and Peninnah. Although Peninnah had children, Hannah did not have any.

Once a year Elkanah traveled from his hometown to Shiloh, where he worshiped the LORD All-Powerful and offered sacrifices. Eli was the LORD's priest there, and his two sons Hophni and Phinehas served with him as priests.

Whenever Elkanah offered a sacrifice, he gave some of the meat to Peninnah and some to each of her sons and daughters. But he gave Hannah even more, because he loved Hannah very much, even though the LORD had kept her from having children of her own.

Peninnah liked to make Hannah feel miserable about not having any children, especially when the family went to the house of the LORD each year.

One day, Elkanah was there offering a sacrifice, when Hannah began crying and refused to eat. So Elkanah asked, "Hannah, why are you crying? Why won't you eat? Why do you feel so bad? Don't I mean more to you than ten sons?"

When the sacrifice had been offered, and they had eaten the meal, Hannah got up and went to pray. Eli was sitting in his chair near the door to the place of worship. Hannah was brokenhearted and was crying as she prayed, "LORD All-Powerful, I am your servant, but I am so miserable! Please let me have a son. I will give him to you for as long as he lives, and his hair will never be cut."

Hannah prayed silently to the LORD for a long time. But her lips were moving, and Eli thought she was drunk. "How long are you going to stay drunk?" he asked. "Sober up!"

"Sir, please don't think I'm no good!" Hannah answered. "I'm not drunk, and I haven't been drinking. But I do feel miserable and terribly upset. I've been praying all this time, telling the LORD about my problems."

Eli replied, "You may go home now and stop worrying. I'm sure the God of Israel will answer your prayer."

"Sir, thank you for being so kind to me," Hannah said. Then she left, and after eating something, she felt much better.

Elkanah and his family got up early the next morning and worshiped the LORD. Then they went back home to Ramah. Later the LORD blessed Elkanah and Hannah with a son. She named him Samuel because she had asked the LORD for him. **(1 SAMUEL 1:1–20 CEV)**

Then the word of the LORD came to him, saying, "Arise, go to Zarephath, which belongs to Sidon, and dwell there. See, I have commanded a widow there to provide for you." So he arose and went to Zarephath. And when he came to the gate of the city, indeed a widow was there gathering sticks. And he called to her and said, "Please bring me a little water in a cup, that I may drink." And as she was going to get it, he called to her and said, "Please bring me a morsel of bread in your hand."

So she said, "As the LORD your God lives, I do not have bread, only a handful of flour in a bin, and a little oil in a jar; and see, I am gathering a couple of sticks that I may go in and prepare it for myself and my son, that we may eat it, and die."

And Elijah said to her, "Do not fear; go and do as you have said, but make me a small cake from it first, and bring it to me; and afterward make some for yourself and your son. For thus says the LORD God of Israel: 'The bin of flour shall not be used up, nor shall the jar of oil run dry, until the day the LORD sends rain on the earth.'"

So she went away and did according to the word of Elijah; and she and he and her household ate for many days. The bin of flour was not used up, nor did the jar of oil run dry, according to the word of the LORD which He spoke by Elijah.

Now it happened after these things that the son of the woman who owned the house became sick. And his sickness was so serious that there was no breath left in him. So she said to Elijah, "What have I to do with you, O man of God? Have you come to me to bring my sin to remembrance, and to kill my son?"

And he said to her, "Give me your son." So he took him out of her arms and carried him to the upper room where he was staying, and laid him on his own bed. Then he cried out to the LORD and said, "O LORD my God, have You also brought tragedy on the widow with whom I lodge, by killing her son?" And he stretched himself out on the child three times, and cried out to the LORD and said, "O LORD my God, I pray, let this child's soul come back to him." Then the LORD heard the voice of Elijah; and the soul of the child came back to him, and he revived.

And Elijah took the child and brought him down from the upper room into the house, and gave him to his mother. And Elijah said, "See, your son lives!"

Then the woman said to Elijah, "Now by this I know that you are a man of God, and that the word of the LORD in your mouth is the truth" **(1 KINGS 17:8–24 NKJV)**.

This miracle by Elijah was later referenced by Jesus in Luke 4 as evidence that God's love extended to all people.

Therefore the LORD Himself will give you a sign: Behold, the virgin shall conceive and bear a Son, and shall call His name Immanuel. **(ISAIAH 7:14 NKJV)**

Now the birth of Jesus Christ was as follows: After His mother Mary was betrothed to Joseph, before they came together, she was found with child of the Holy Spirit. Then

Joseph her husband, being a just man, and not wanting to make her a public example, was minded to put her away secretly. But while he thought about these things, behold, an angel of the Lord appeared to him in a dream, saying, "Joseph, son of David, do not be afraid to take to you Mary your wife, for that which is conceived in her is of the Holy Spirit. And she will bring forth a Son, and you shall call His name JESUS, for He will save His people from their sins."

So all this was done that it might be fulfilled which was spoken by the Lord through the prophet, saying: "Behold, the virgin shall be with child, and bear a Son, and they shall call His name Immanuel," which is translated, "God with us."

Then Joseph, being aroused from sleep, did as the angel of the Lord commanded him and took to him his wife, and did not know her till she had brought forth her firstborn Son. And he called His name JESUS. (MATTHEW 1:18–25 NKJV)

Jesus left that place and went to the area of Tyre and Sidon. A Canaanite woman from that area came to Jesus and cried out, "Lord, Son of David, have mercy on me! My daughter has a demon, and she is suffering very much."

But Jesus did not answer the woman. So his followers came to Jesus and begged him, "Tell the woman to go away. She is following us and shouting." Jesus answered, "God sent me only to the lost sheep, the people of Israel."

Then the woman came to Jesus again and bowed before him and said, "Lord, help me!"

Jesus answered, "It is not right to take the children's bread and give it to the dogs."

The woman said, "Yes, Lord, but even the dogs eat the crumbs that fall from their masters' table."

Then Jesus answered, "Woman, you have great faith! I will do what you asked." And at that moment the woman's daughter was healed. (MATTHEW 15:21-28 NCV)

After Jesus crossed over by boat, a large crowd met him at the seaside. One of the meeting-place leaders named Jairus came. When he saw Jesus, he fell to his knees, beside himself as he begged, "My dear daughter is at death's door. Come and lay hands on her so she will get well and live." Jesus went with him, the whole crowd tagging along, pushing and jostling him.

A woman who had suffered a condition of hemorrhaging for twelve years—a long succession of physicians had treated her, and treated her badly, taking all her money and leaving her worse off than before—had heard about Jesus. She slipped in from behind and touched his robe. She was thinking to herself, "If I can put a finger on his robe, I can get well." The moment she did it, the flow of blood dried up. She could feel the change and knew her plague was over and done with.

At the same moment, Jesus felt energy discharging from him. He turned around to the crowd and asked, "Who touched my robe?"

His disciples said, "What are you talking about? With this crowd pushing and jostling you, you're asking, 'Who touched me?' Dozens have touched you!"

But he went on asking, looking around to see who had done it. The woman, knowing what had happened, knowing she was the one, stepped up in fear and trembling, knelt before him, and gave him the whole story.

Jesus said to her, "Daughter, you took a risk of faith, and now you're healed and whole. Live well, live blessed! Be healed of your plague."

While he was still talking, some people came from the leader's house and told him, "Your daughter is dead. Why bother the Teacher any more?"

Jesus overheard what they were talking about and said to the leader, "Don't listen to them; just trust me."

He permitted no one to go in with him except Peter, James, and John. They entered the leader's house and pushed their way through the gossips looking for a story and neighbors bringing in casseroles. Jesus was abrupt: "Why all this busybody grief and gossip? This child isn't dead; she's sleeping." Provoked to sarcasm, they told him he didn't know what he was talking about.

But when he had sent them all out, he took the child's father and mother, along with his companions, and entered the child's room. He clasped the girl's hand and said, "Talitha koum," which means, "Little girl, get up." At that, she was up and walking around! This girl was twelve years of age. They, of course, were all beside themselves with joy. He gave them strict orders that no one was to know what had taken place in that room. Then he said, "Give her something to eat" (MARK 5:21–43 THE MESSAGE).

When Jesus and his three disciples came back down, they saw a large crowd around the other disciples. The teachers of the Law of Moses were arguing with them.

The crowd was really surprised to see Jesus, and everyone hurried over to greet him.

Jesus asked, "What are you arguing about?"

Someone from the crowd answered, "Teacher, I brought my son to you. A demon keeps him from talking. Whenever the demon attacks my son, it throws him to the ground and makes him foam at the mouth and grit his teeth in pain. Then he becomes stiff. I asked your disciples to force out the demon, but they couldn't do it."

Jesus said, "You people don't have any faith! How much longer must I be with you? Why do I have to put up with you? Bring the boy to me."

They brought the boy, and as soon as the demon saw Jesus, it made the boy shake all over. He fell down and began rolling on the ground and foaming at the mouth.

Jesus asked the boy's father, "How long has he been like this?"

The man answered, "Ever since he was a child. The demon has often tried to kill him by throwing him into a fire or into water. Please have pity and help us if you can!"

Jesus replied, "Why do you say 'if you can'? Anything is possible for someone who has faith!"

Right away the boy's father shouted, "I do have faith! Please help me to have even more."

When Jesus saw that a crowd was gathering fast, he spoke sternly to the evil spirit that had kept the boy from speaking or hearing. He said, "I order you to come out of the boy! Don't ever bother him again."

The spirit screamed and made the boy shake all over. Then it went out of him. The boy looked dead, and almost everyone said he was. But Jesus took hold of his hand and helped him stand up.

After Jesus and the disciples had gone back home and were alone, they asked him, "Why couldn't we force out that demon?"

Jesus answered, "Only prayer can force out that kind of demon" (MARK 9:14–29 CEV).

Satan—and the world that has fallen under his influence—attacks children every bit as much as he does adults.

In the time of Herod king of Judea there was a priest named Zechariah, who belonged to the priestly division of Abijah; his wife Elizabeth was also a descendant of Aaron. Both of them were righteous in the sight of God, observing all the Lord's commands and decrees blamelessly. But they were childless because Elizabeth was not able to conceive, and they were both very old.

Once when Zechariah's division was on duty and he was serving as priest before God, he was chosen by lot, according to the custom of the priesthood, to go into the temple of the Lord and burn incense. And when the time for the burning of incense came, all the assembled worshipers were praying outside.

Then an angel of the Lord appeared to him, standing at the right side of the altar of incense. When Zechariah saw him, he was startled and was gripped with fear. But the angel said to him: "Do not be afraid, Zechariah; your prayer has been heard. Your wife Elizabeth will bear you a son, and you are to call him John. He will be a joy and delight to you, and many will rejoice because of his birth, for he will be great in the sight of the Lord. He is never to take wine or other fermented drink, and he will be filled with the Holy Spirit even before he is born. He will bring back many of the people of Israel to the Lord their God. And he will go on before the Lord, in the spirit and power of Elijah, to turn the hearts of the parents to their children and the disobedient to the wisdom of the righteous—to make ready a people prepared for the Lord." Zechariah asked the angel, "How can I be sure of this? I am an old man and my wife is well along in years." The angel said to him, "I am Gabriel. I stand in the presence of God, and I have been sent to speak to you and to tell you this good news. And now you will be silent and not able to speak until the day this happens, because you did not believe my words, which will come true at their appointed time."

Meanwhile, the people were waiting for Zechariah and wondering why he stayed so long in the temple. When he came out, he could not speak to them. They realized he had seen a vision in the temple, for he kept making signs to them but remained unable to speak. When his time of service was completed, he returned home. After this his wife Elizabeth became pregnant and for five months remained in seclusion. "The Lord has done this for me," she said. "In these days he has shown his favor and taken away my disgrace among the people." . . .

When it was time for Elizabeth to have her baby, she gave birth to a son. Her neighbors and relatives heard that the Lord had shown her great mercy, and they shared her joy.

On the eighth day they came to circumcise the child, and they were going to name him after his father Zechariah, but his mother spoke up and said, "No! He is to be called John."

They said to her, "There is no one among your relatives who has that name."

Then they made signs to his father, to find out what he would like to name the child. He asked for a writing tablet, and to everyone's astonishment he wrote, "His name is John." Immediately his mouth was opened and his tongue set free, and he began to speak, praising God. All the neighbors were filled with awe, and throughout the hill country of Judea people were talking about all these things. Everyone who heard this wondered about it, asking, "What then is this child going to be?" For the Lord's hand was with him. (LUKE 1:5–25, 57–66 NIV)

Not long after that, Jesus went to the village Nain. His disciples were with him, along with quite a large crowd. As they approached the village gate, they met a funeral procession—a woman's only son was being carried out for burial. And the mother was a widow. When Jesus saw her, his heart broke. He said to her, "Don't cry." Then he went over and touched the coffin. The pallbearers stopped. He said, "Young man, I tell you: Get up." The dead son sat up and began talking. Jesus presented him to his mother.

They all realized they were in a place of holy mystery, that God was at work among them. They were quietly worshipful—and then noisily grateful, calling out among themselves, "God is back, looking to the needs of his people!" The news of Jesus spread all through the country. (LUKE 7:11–17 THE MESSAGE)

So he came again to Cana in Galilee, where he had made the water wine. And at Capernaum there was an official whose son was ill. When this man heard that Jesus had come from Judea to Galilee, he went to him and asked him to come down and heal his son, for he was at the point of death. So Jesus said to him, "Unless you see signs and wonders you will not believe." The official said to him, "Sir, come down before my child dies." Jesus said to him, "Go; your son will live." The man believed the word that Jesus spoke to him and went on his way. As he was going down, his servants met him and told him that his son was recovering. So he asked them the hour when he began to get better, and they said to him, "Yesterday at the seventh hour the fever left him." The father knew that was the hour when Jesus had said to him, "Your son will live." And he himself believed, and all his household. This was now the second sign that Jesus did when he had come from Judea to Galilee. (JOHN 4:46–54 ESV)

———

One day, on our way to the place of prayer, a slave girl ran into us. She was a psychic and, with her fortunetelling, made a lot of money for the people who owned her. She started following Paul around, calling everyone's attention to us by yelling out, "These men are working for the Most High God. They're laying out the road of salvation for you!" She did this for a number of days until Paul, finally fed up with her, turned and commanded the spirit that possessed her, "Out! In the name of Jesus Christ, get out of her!" And it was gone, just like that.

When her owners saw that their lucrative little business was suddenly bankrupt, they went after Paul and Silas, roughed them up and dragged them into the market square. Then the police arrested them and pulled them into a court with the accusation, "These men are disturbing the peace—dangerous

Jewish agitators subverting our Roman law and order." By this time the crowd had turned into a restless mob out for blood.

The judges went along with the mob, had Paul and Silas's clothes ripped off and ordered a public beating. After beating them black-and-blue, they threw them into jail, telling the jailkeeper to put them under heavy guard so there would be no chance of escape. He did just that—threw them into the maximum security cell in the jail and clamped leg irons on them.

Along about midnight, Paul and Silas were at prayer and singing a robust hymn to God. The other prisoners couldn't believe their ears. Then, without warning, a huge earthquake! The jailhouse tottered, every door flew open, all the prisoners were loose.

Startled from sleep, the jailer saw all the doors swinging loose on their hinges. Assuming that all the prisoners had escaped, he pulled out his sword and was about to do himself in, figuring he was as good as dead anyway, when Paul stopped him: "Don't do that! We're all still here! Nobody's run away!"

The jailer got a torch and ran inside. Badly shaken, he collapsed in front of Paul and Silas. He led them out of the jail and asked, "Sirs, what do I have to do to be saved, to really live?" They said, "Put your entire trust in the Master Jesus. Then you'll live as you were meant to live—and everyone in your house included!"

They went on to spell out in detail the story of the Master—the entire family got in on this part. They never did get to bed that night. The jailer made them feel at home, dressed their wounds, and then—he couldn't wait till morning!—was baptized, he and everyone in his family. There in his home, he had food set out for a festive meal. It was a night to remember: He and his entire family had put their trust in God; everyone in the house was in on the celebration.

At daybreak, the court judges sent officers with the instructions, "Release these men." The jailer gave Paul the message, "The judges sent word that you're free to go on your way. Congratulations! Go in peace!" But Paul wouldn't budge. He told the officers, "They beat us up in public and threw us in jail, Roman citizens in good standing! And now they want to get us out of the way on the sly without anyone knowing? Nothing doing! If they want us out of here, let them come themselves and lead us out in broad daylight." When the officers reported this, the judges panicked. They had no idea that Paul and Silas were Roman citizens. They hurried over and apologized, personally escorted them from the jail, and then asked them if they wouldn't please leave the city. Walking out of the jail, Paul and Silas went straight to Lydia's house, saw their friends again, encouraged them in the faith, and only then went on their way. (ACTS 16:16–40 THE MESSAGE)

7

Children and Faith

And this is one thing, wherein it is necessary we should become as little children, in order to our entering into the kingdom of God, even that we should have our hearts tender, and easily affected and moved in spiritual and divine things, as little children have in other things.[10]

Jonathan Edwards

Children have capabilities far greater than adults in many ways. Take their physical makeup, for example. A little boy or a little girl is running down the sidewalk and skins their knee. They cry, Mommy kisses it and puts a Band-Aid on it, and they are back running down the sidewalk again in no time. If an adult did the same thing, they would be limping for days. Consider the flexibility of small children. Just one time, try mimicking an infant as they literally put their foot in their mouth. Trying to do the same thing any way but metaphorically will probably leave the average adult with a torn muscle, stuck looking like a human pretzel, and calling 9-1-1.

In much the same way that children have greater capacities than adults, who are much larger and stronger, they also have some spiritual capabilities that far outstretch those of their parents, grandparents, and other adults. A child believes in God and his Word, unfettered by doubts and struggles to believe that are so common among those who have been alive for decades. Adults struggle to believe God because life, the world, and the devil have spent years telling them that God cannot be trusted. A child, however, believes God without all of the clutter and difficulties of adulthood.

So the next time you see a child pulling their leg over their head, don't grimace—let it stretch your faith.

—◦◦◦—

The boy Samuel was serving GOD under Eli's direction. This was at a time when the revelation of GOD was rarely heard or seen. One night Eli was sound asleep (his eyesight was very bad—he could hardly see). It was well before dawn; the sanctuary lamp was still burning. Samuel was still in bed in the Temple of GOD, where the Chest of God rested.

Then GOD called out, "Samuel, Samuel!"

Samuel answered, "Yes? I'm here." Then he ran to Eli saying, "I heard you call. Here I am."

Eli said, "I didn't call you. Go back to bed." And so he did.

GOD called again, "Samuel, Samuel!" Samuel got up and went to Eli, "I heard you call. Here I am."

Again Eli said, "Son, I didn't call you. Go back to bed." (This all happened before Samuel knew GOD for himself.

It was before the revelation of GOD had been given to him personally.)

GOD called again, "Samuel!"—the third time! Yet again Samuel got up and went to Eli, "Yes? I heard you call me. Here I am."

That's when it dawned on Eli that GOD was calling the boy. So Eli directed Samuel, "Go back and lie down. If the voice calls again, say, 'Speak, GOD. I'm your servant, ready to listen.'" Samuel returned to his bed.

Then GOD came and stood before him exactly as before, calling out, "Samuel! Samuel!"

Samuel answered, "Speak. I'm your servant, ready to listen."

GOD said to Samuel, "Listen carefully. I'm getting ready to do something in Israel that is going to shake everyone up and get their attention. The time has come for me to bring down on Eli's family everything I warned him of, every last word of it. I'm letting him know that the time's up. I'm bringing judgment on his family for good. He knew what was going on, that his sons were desecrating God's name and God's place, and he did nothing to stop them. This is my sentence on the family of Eli: The evil of Eli's family can never be wiped out by sacrifice or offering."

Samuel stayed in bed until morning, then rose early and went about his duties, opening the doors of the sanctuary, but he dreaded having to tell the vision to Eli.

But then Eli summoned Samuel: "Samuel, my son!"

Samuel came running: "Yes? What can I do for you?"

"What did he say? Tell it to me, all of it. Don't suppress or soften one word, as God is your judge! I want it all, word for word as he said it to you."

So Samuel told him, word for word. He held back nothing. Eli said, "He is GOD. Let him do whatever he thinks best."

Samuel grew up. GOD was with him, and Samuel's prophetic record was flawless. Everyone in Israel, from Dan in the north to Beersheba in the south, recognized that Samuel was the real thing—a true prophet of GOD. GOD continued to show up at Shiloh, revealed through his word to Samuel at Shiloh. (1 SAMUEL 3:1–21 THE MESSAGE)

Not only was Samuel's birth a miracle in and of itself, but he lived a life of faith on his own, even as a child.

Now Naaman, captain of the army of the king of Aram, was a great man with his master, and highly respected, because by him the LORD had given victory to Aram. The man was also a valiant warrior, but he was a leper. Now the Arameans had gone out in bands and had taken captive a little girl from the land of Israel; and she waited on Naaman's wife. She said to her mistress, "I wish that my master were with the prophet who is in Samaria! Then he would cure him of his leprosy." Naaman went in and told his master, saying, "Thus and thus spoke the girl who is from the land of Israel." Then the king of Aram said, "Go now, and I will send a letter to the king of Israel." He departed and took with him ten talents of silver and six thousand shekels of gold and ten changes of clothes.

He brought the letter to the king of Israel, saying, "And now as this letter comes to you, behold, I have sent Naaman my servant to you, that you may cure him of his leprosy." When the king of Israel read the letter, he tore his clothes and said, "Am I God, to kill and to make alive, that this man is sending word to me to cure a man of his leprosy? But consider now, and see how he is seeking a quarrel against me."

It happened when Elisha the man of God heard that the king of Israel had torn his clothes, that he sent word to the king, saying, "Why have you torn your clothes? Now let him come to me, and he shall know that there is a prophet in Israel." So Naaman came with his horses and his chariots and stood at the doorway of the house of Elisha. Elisha sent a messenger to him, saying, "Go and wash in the Jordan seven times, and your flesh will be restored to you and you will be clean." But Naaman was furious and went away and said, "Behold, I thought, 'He will surely come out to me and stand and call on the name of the LORD his God, and wave his hand over the place and cure the leper.' "Are not Abanah and Pharpar, the rivers of Damascus, better than all the waters of Israel? Could I not wash in them and be clean?" So he turned and went away in a rage. Then his servants came near and spoke to him and said, "My father, had the prophet told you to do some great thing, would you not have done it? How much more then, when he says to you, 'Wash, and be clean'?" So he went down and dipped himself seven times in the Jordan, according to the word of the man of God; and his flesh was restored like the flesh of a little child and he was clean. (2 KINGS 5:1–14 NASB)

Josiah was eight years old when he began to reign, and he reigned thirty-one years in Jerusalem. And he did what was right in the eyes of the LORD, and walked in the ways of David his father; and he did not turn aside to the right hand or to the left. For in the eighth year of his reign, while he was yet a boy, he began to seek the God of David his father, and in the twelfth year he began to purge Judah and Jerusalem of the high places, the Asherim, and the carved and the metal images. And they chopped down the altars of the Baals in his presence, and he cut down the incense altars that stood above them. And he broke in pieces the Asherim and the carved and the metal images, and he made dust of them and scattered it over the graves of those who had sacrificed to them. (2 CHRONICLES 34:1–4 ESV)

Josiah, at sixteen years of age, showed more character and integrity than almost any other king of Israel or Judah.

I run to you, LORD, for protection. Don't disappoint me. You do what is right, so come to my rescue. Listen to my prayer and keep me safe. Be my mighty rock, the place where I can always run for protection. Save me by your command! You are my mighty rock and my fortress.

Come and save me, LORD God, from vicious and cruel and brutal enemies! I depend on you, and I have trusted you since I was young. I have relied on you from the day I was born. You brought me safely through birth, and I always praise you. (PSALM 71:1–6 CEV)

And the word of the LORD of hosts came to me, saying,

Thus says the LORD of hosts: I am jealous for Zion with great jealousy, and I am jealous for her with great wrath [against her enemies].

Thus says the LORD: I shall return to Zion and will dwell in the midst of Jerusalem, and Jerusalem shall be called the [faithful] City of Truth, and the mountain of the LORD of hosts, the Holy Mountain.

Thus says the LORD of hosts: Old men and old women shall again dwell in Jerusalem and sit out in the streets, every man with his staff in his hand for very [advanced] age.

And the streets of the city shall be full of boys and girls playing in its streets. **(ZECHARIAH 8:1-5 AMP)**

God's promise of a future millennium included a time so peaceful that it would be signified by streets full of children playing.

Then some children were brought to Him so that He might lay His hands on them and pray; and the disciples rebuked them. But Jesus said, "Let the children alone, and do not hinder them from coming to Me; for the kingdom of heaven belongs to such as these." After laying His hands on them, He departed from there. **(MATTHEW 19:13-15 NASB)**

And the blind and the lame came to him in the temple, and he healed them. But when the chief priests and the scribes saw the wonderful things that he did, and the children crying out in the temple, "Hosanna to the Son of David!" they were indignant, and they said to him, "Do you hear what these are saying?" And Jesus said to them, "Yes, have you never read, 'Out of the mouth of infants and nursing babies you have prepared praise'?" **(MATTHEW 21:14-16 ESV)**.

Every year Jesus' parents went to Jerusalem for the Passover festival. When Jesus was twelve years old, they attended the festival as usual. After the celebration was over, they started home to Nazareth, but Jesus stayed behind in Jerusalem. His parents didn't miss him at first, because they assumed he was among the other travelers. But when he didn't show up that evening, they started looking for him among their relatives and friends. When they couldn't find him, they went back to Jerusalem to search for him there.

Three days later they finally discovered him in the Temple, sitting among the religious teachers, listening to them and asking questions. All who heard him were amazed at his understanding and his answers.

His parents didn't know what to think. "Son," his mother said to him, "why have you done this to us? Your father and I have been frantic, searching for you everywhere."

"But why did you need to search?" he asked. "Didn't you know that I must be in my Father's house?" But they didn't understand what he meant.

Then he returned to Nazareth with them and was obedient to them. And his mother stored all these things in her heart.

Jesus grew in wisdom and in stature and in favor with God and all the people. (LUKE 2:41–52 NLT)

After this, Jesus crossed over to the far side of the Sea of Galilee, also known as the Sea of Tiberias. A huge crowd kept following him wherever he went, because they saw his miraculous signs as he healed the sick. Then Jesus climbed a hill and sat down with his disciples around him. (It was nearly time for the Jewish Passover celebration.) Jesus soon saw a huge crowd of people coming to look for him. Turning to Philip, he asked, "Where can we buy bread to feed all these people?" He was testing Philip, for he already knew what he was going to do.

Philip replied, "Even if we worked for months, we wouldn't have enough money to feed them!"

Then Andrew, Simon Peter's brother, spoke up. "There's a young boy here with five barley loaves and two fish. But what good is that with this huge crowd?"

"Tell everyone to sit down," Jesus said. So they all sat down on the grassy slopes. (The men alone numbered about 5,000.) Then Jesus took the loaves, gave thanks to God, and distributed them to the people. Afterward he did the same with the fish. And they all ate as much as they wanted. After everyone was full, Jesus told his disciples, "Now gather the leftovers, so that nothing is wasted." So they picked up the pieces and filled twelve baskets with scraps left by the people who had eaten from the five barley loaves.

When the people saw him do this miraculous sign, they exclaimed, "Surely, he is the Prophet we have been expecting!" When Jesus saw that they were ready to force him to be their king, he slipped away into the hills by himself. (JOHN 6:1-15 NLT)

But as for you, continue to hold to the things that you have learned and of which you are convinced, knowing from whom you learned [them],

And how from your childhood you have had a knowledge of and been acquainted with the sacred Writings, which are able to instruct you and give you the understanding for salvation which comes through faith in Christ Jesus [through the leaning of the entire human personality on God in Christ Jesus in absolute trust and confidence in His power, wisdom, and goodness]. (2 TIMOTHY 3:14-15 AMP)

Timothy learned the Scriptures as a small child. He learned them from his godly mother and grandmother. Most often faith is passed on from one generation to another.

8

God, the Perfect Father

It is much easier to become a father than to be one.[11]

Kent Nerburn

Parents are tasked with doing an almost impossible job: raising and training another human being to be a responsible, functioning member of society. Parents who are believers have an additional difficult task: disciplining and training their children in the faith. While parents are a child's first role model in the world, they unfortunately have the innate bad habit of passing along their own flaws and faults to their children.

Even the best parents need help overcoming their own weaknesses. No matter how old they are or how much experience they have, parents still need their heavenly Father.

The presence of God the Father not only comforts earthly parents, it also lights the path of a better way.

~~~

And the LORD said to Moses, "When you go back to Egypt, see that you do before Pharaoh all the miracles that I have put in your power. But I will harden his heart, so that he will not let the people go. Then you shall say to Pharaoh, 'Thus says the LORD, Israel is my firstborn son, and I say to you, "Let my son go that he may serve me." If you refuse to let him go, behold, I will kill your firstborn son'" (EXODUS 4:21–23 NASB).

They have corrupted themselves; they are not his children, because of their blemish: A perverse and crooked generation. Do you thus deal with the LORD, O foolish and unwise people? Is He not your Father, who bought you? Has He not made you and established you? (DEUTERONOMY 32:5–6 NKJV)

Sing to God; sing praises to his name. Prepare the way for him who rides through the desert, whose name is the LORD. Rejoice before him. God is in his holy Temple. He is a father to orphans, and he defends the widows. God gives the lonely a home. He leads prisoners out with joy, but those who turn against God will live in a dry land. (PSALM 68:4–6 NCV)

LORD, look down from heaven; look from your holy, glorious home, and see us. Where is the passion and the might you used to show on our behalf? Where are your mercy and compassion now? Surely you are still our Father! Even if Abraham and Jacob would disown us, LORD, you would still be our Father.

You are our Redeemer from ages past. LORD, why have you allowed us to turn from your path? Why have you given us stubborn hearts so we no longer fear you? Return and help us, for we are your servants, the tribes that are your special possession. How briefly your holy people possessed your holy place, and now our enemies have destroyed it. Sometimes it seems as though we never belonged to you, as though we had never been known as your people. (ISAIAH 63:15–19 NLT)

You, LORD, are our Father. We are nothing but clay, but you are the potter who molded us. Don't be so furious or keep our sins in your thoughts forever! Remember that all of us are your people. (ISAIAH 64:8–9 CEV)

You are the salt of the earth. But if the salt loses its saltiness, how can it be made salty again? It is no longer good for anything, except to be thrown out and trampled underfoot.

You are the light of the world. A town built on a hill cannot be hidden. Neither do people light a lamp and put it under a bowl. Instead they put it on its stand, and it gives light to everyone in the house. In the same way, let your light shine before others, that they may see your good deeds and glorify your Father in heaven. (MATTHEW 5:13–16 NIV)

You have heard that it was said, "Love your neighbor and hate your enemy." But I tell you, love your enemies and pray for those who persecute you, that you may be children of your Father in heaven. He causes his sun to rise on the evil and the good, and sends rain on the righteous and the unrighteous. If you love those who love you, what reward will you get?

Are not even the tax collectors doing that? And if you greet only your own people, what are you doing more than others? Do not even pagans do that? Be perfect, therefore, as your heavenly Father is perfect. (MATTHEW 5:43–48 NIV)

God the Father is more than just a good example for parents; he is the standard of perfection that all are judged against.

Be especially careful when you are trying to be good so that you don't make a performance out of it. It might be good theater, but the God who made you won't be applauding. When you do something for someone else, don't call attention to yourself. You've seen them in action, I'm sure—"playactors" I call them—treating prayer meeting and street corner alike as a stage, acting compassionate as long as someone is watching, playing to the crowds. They get applause, true, but that's all they get. When you help someone out, don't think about how it looks. Just do it—quietly and unobtrusively. That is the way your God, who conceived you in love, working behind the scenes, helps you out.

"And when you come before God, don't turn that into a theatrical production either. All these people making a regular show out of their prayers, hoping for stardom! Do you think God sits in a box seat?

Here's what I want you to do: Find a quiet, secluded place so you won't be tempted to role-play before God. Just be there as simply and honestly as you can manage. The focus will shift from you to God, and you will begin to sense his grace.

The world is full of so-called prayer warriors who are prayer-ignorant. They're full of formulas and programs and advice, peddling techniques for getting what you want from

God. Don't fall for that nonsense. This is your Father you are dealing with, and he knows better than you what you need. With a God like this loving you, you can pray very simply. Like this:

> Our Father in heaven,
> Reveal who you are.
> Set the world right;
> Do what's best—as above, so below.
> Keep us alive with three square meals.
> Keep us forgiven with you and forgiving others.
> Keep us safe from ourselves and the Devil.
> You're in charge!
> You can do anything you want!
> You're ablaze in beauty!
> > Yes. Yes. Yes.

In prayer there is a connection between what God does and what you do. You can't get forgiveness from God, for instance, without also forgiving others. If you refuse to do your part, you cut yourself off from God's part. When you practice some appetite-denying discipline to better concentrate on God, don't make a production out of it. It might turn you into a small-time celebrity but it won't make you a saint. If you "go into training" inwardly, act normal outwardly. Shampoo and comb your hair, brush your teeth, wash your face. God doesn't require attention-getting devices. He won't overlook what you are doing; he'll reward you well. **(MATTHEW 6:1–18 THE MESSAGE)**

Ask, and you will receive. Search, and you will find. Knock, and the door will be opened for you. Everyone who asks will receive. Everyone who searches will find. And the door will be opened for everyone who knocks. Would any of you give your hungry child a stone, if the child asked for some bread? Would you give your child a snake if the child asked for a fish? As bad as you are, you still know how to give good gifts to your children. But your heavenly Father is even more ready to give good things to people who ask.

Treat others as you want them to treat you. This is what the Law and the Prophets are all about. (MATTHEW 7:7–12 CEV)

Not everyone who says to Me, Lord, Lord, will enter the kingdom of heaven, but he who does the will of My Father Who is in heaven.

Many will say to Me on that day, Lord, Lord, have we not prophesied in Your name and driven out demons in Your name and done many mighty works in Your name?

And then I will say to them openly (publicly), I never knew you; depart from Me, you who act wickedly [disregarding My commands]. (MATTHEW 7:21–23 AMP)

At that time Jesus said, "I praise You, Father, Lord of heaven and earth, that You have hidden these things from the wise and intelligent and have revealed them to infants. Yes, Father, for this way was well-pleasing in Your sight. All things have been handed over to Me by My Father; and no one knows the Son except the Father; nor does anyone know the Father except the Son, and anyone to whom the Son wills to reveal Him.

"Come to Me, all who are weary and heavy-laden, and I will give you rest. Take My yoke upon you and learn from Me, for I am gentle and humble in heart, and YOU WILL FIND REST FOR YOUR SOULS. For My yoke is easy and My burden is light" (MATTHEW 11:25–30 NASB).

God as the all-knowing creator of his children always knows just what to tell them and when.

While Jesus was still talking to the crowd, his mother and brothers stood outside, wanting to speak to him. Someone told him, "Your mother and brothers are standing outside, wanting to speak to you."

He replied to him, "Who is my mother, and who are my brothers?" Pointing to his disciples, he said, "Here are my mother and my brothers. For whoever does the will of my Father in heaven is my brother and sister and mother" (MATTHEW 12:46–50 NIV).

Watch that you don't treat a single one of these childlike believers arrogantly. You realize, don't you, that their personal angels are constantly in touch with my Father in heaven?

Look at it this way. If someone has a hundred sheep and one of them wanders off, doesn't he leave the ninety-nine and go after the one? And if he finds it, doesn't he make far more over it than over the ninety-nine who stay put? Your Father in heaven feels the same way. He doesn't want to lose even one of these simple believers.

If a fellow believer hurts you, go and tell him—work it out between the two of you. If he listens, you've made a friend. If he won't listen, take one or two others along so that the presence of witnesses will keep things honest, and try again. If he still won't listen, tell the church. If he won't listen to the church, you'll have to start over from scratch, confront him with the need for repentance, and offer again God's forgiving love.

Take this most seriously: A yes on earth is yes in heaven; a no on earth is no in heaven. What you say to one another is eternal. I mean this. When two of you get together on anything at all on earth and make a prayer of it, my Father in heaven goes into action. And when two or three of you are together because of me, you can be sure that I'll be there. **(MATTHEW 18:10–20 THE MESSAGE)**

Jesus told his disciples:

Have faith in God! If you have faith in God and don't doubt, you can tell this mountain to get up and jump into the sea, and it will. Everything you ask for in prayer will be yours, if you only have faith.

Whenever you stand up to pray, you must forgive what others have done to you. Then your Father in heaven will forgive your sins. **(MARK 11:22–26 CEV)**

But to you who are willing to listen, I say, love your enemies! Do good to those who hate you. Bless those who curse you. Pray for those who hurt you. If someone slaps you on one cheek, offer the other cheek also. If someone demands your coat, offer your shirt also. Give to anyone who asks; and when things are taken away from you, don't try to get them back. Do to others as you would like them to do to you.

If you love only those who love you, why should you get credit for that? Even sinners love those who love them! And if you do good only to those who do good to you, why should you get credit? Even sinners do that much! And if you lend money only to those who can repay you, why should you get credit? Even sinners will lend to other sinners for a full return.

Love your enemies! Do good to them. Lend to them without expecting to be repaid. Then your reward from heaven will be very great, and you will truly be acting as children of the Most High, for he is kind to those who are unthankful and wicked. You must be compassionate, just as your Father is compassionate. (LUKE 6:27–36 NLT)

At that time Jesus, full of joy through the Holy Spirit, said, "I praise you, Father, Lord of heaven and earth, because you have hidden these things from the wise and learned, and revealed them to little children. Yes, Father, for this is what you were pleased to do.

"All things have been committed to me by my Father. No one knows who the Son is except the Father, and no one knows who the Father is except the Son and those to whom the Son chooses to reveal him."

Then he turned to his disciples and said privately, "Blessed are the eyes that see what you see. For I tell you that many prophets and kings wanted to see what you see but did not see it, and to hear what you hear but did not hear it" (LUKE 10:21–24 NIV).

Consider the lilies, how they grow. They neither [wearily] toil nor spin nor weave; yet I tell you, even Solomon in all his glory (his splendor and magnificence) was not arrayed like one of these.

But if God so clothes the grass in the field, which is alive today, and tomorrow is thrown into the furnace, how much more will He clothe you, O you [people] of little faith?

And you, do not seek [by meditating and reasoning to inquire into] what you are to eat and what you are to drink;

nor be of anxious (troubled) mind [unsettled, excited, worried, and in suspense];

For all the pagan world is [greedily] seeking these things, and your Father knows that you need them.

Only aim at and strive for and seek His kingdom, and all these things shall be supplied to you also. (LUKE 12:27–31 AMP)

"This is what I want you to do: Ask the Father for whatever is in keeping with the things I've revealed to you. Ask in my name, according to my will, and he'll most certainly give it to you. Your joy will be a river overflowing its banks! I've used figures of speech in telling you these things. Soon I'll drop the figures and tell you about the Father in plain language. Then you can make your requests directly to him in relation to this life I've revealed to you. I won't continue making requests of the Father on your behalf. I won't need to. Because you've gone out on a limb, committed yourselves to love and trust in me, believing I came directly from the Father, the Father loves you directly. First, I left the Father and arrived in the world; now I leave the world and travel to the Father."

His disciples said, "Finally! You're giving it to us straight, in plain talk—no more figures of speech. Now we know that you know everything—it all comes together in you. You won't have to put up with our questions anymore. We're convinced you came from God."

Jesus answered them, "Do you finally believe? In fact, you're about to make a run for it—saving your own skins and abandoning me. But I'm not abandoned. The Father is with me. I've told you all this so that trusting me, you will be unshakable and assured, deeply at peace. In this godless world you will continue to experience difficulties. But take heart! I've conquered the world" (JOHN 16:23–33 THE MESSAGE).

So then, brothers, we are debtors, not to the flesh, to live according to the flesh. For if you live according to the flesh you will die, but if by the Spirit you put to death the deeds of the body, you will live. For all who are led by the Spirit of God are sons of God. For you did not receive the spirit of slavery to fall back into fear, but you have received the Spirit of adoption as sons, by whom we cry, "Abba! Father!" The Spirit himself bears witness with our spirit that we are children of God, and if children, then heirs—heirs of God and fellow heirs with Christ, provided we suffer with him in order that we may also be glorified with him. (ROMANS 8:12–17 ESV)

Praise God, the Father of our Lord Jesus Christ! The Father is a merciful God, who always gives us comfort. He comforts us when we are in trouble, so that we can share that same comfort with others in trouble. We share in the terrible sufferings of Christ, but also in the wonderful comfort he gives. We suffer in the hope that you will be comforted and saved. And because we are comforted, you will also be comforted, as you patiently endure suffering like ours. You never disappoint us. You suffered as much as we did, and we know that you will be comforted as we were. (2 CORINTHIANS 1:3–7 CEV)

Do not be unequally yoked together with unbelievers. For what fellowship has righteousness with lawlessness? And what communion has light with darkness? And what accord has Christ with Belial? Or what part has a believer with an unbeliever? And what agreement has the temple of God with idols? For you are the temple of the living God. As God has said: "I will dwell in them and walk among them. I will be their God, and they shall be My people." Therefore "Come out from among them and be separate, says the Lord. Do not touch what is unclean, and I will receive you. I will be a Father to you, and you shall be My sons and daughters, says the Lord Almighty." **(2 CORINTHIANS 6:14–18 NKJV)**

Do not be deceived, my beloved brethren. Every good thing given and every perfect gift is from above, coming down from the Father of lights, with whom there is no variation or shifting shadow. In the exercise of His will He brought us forth by the word of truth, so that we would be a kind of first fruits among His creatures. **(JAMES 1:16–18 NASB)**

But as the One Who called you is holy, you yourselves also be holy in all your conduct and manner of living. For it is written, You shall be holy, for I am holy. And if you call upon Him as [your] Father Who judges each one impartially according to what he does, [then] you should conduct yourselves with true reverence throughout the time of your temporary residence [on the earth, whether long or short]. **(1 PETER 1:15–17 AMP)**

Do not love the world or the things in the world. If anyone loves the world, the love of the Father is not in him. For all that is in the world—the desires of the flesh and the desires of the eyes and pride in possessions—is not from the Father but is from the world. And the world is passing away along with its desires, but whoever does the will of God abides forever. **(1 JOHN 2:15–17 ESV)**

9

Jesus, the Perfect Son

~~~~~

God had one son on earth without sin, but never one without suffering.[12]

Saint Augustine

Some siblings are very close. Others fall just short of mortal enemies. Sometimes they are both.

Some siblings (such as football's Mannings—Peyton and Eli) spend a lifetime following in one another's footsteps. Others, such as Roger, the younger brother of President Bill Clinton, are a source of constant embarrassment. Sibling rivalries and difficulties are as old as the first siblings, Cain and Abel. Those two sons of Adam and Eve experienced a rift so deep that the first sibling relationship led to the first murder. Many with siblings can sympathize.

Thankfully our heavenly family has a few differences from our earthly ones. Unlike our earthly siblings whom we admire and emulate only to discover their flaws, Jesus Christ is the perfect example of an older brother. In fact, God's plan was for all believers to be "conformed to the image of his Son, so that he might be the firstborn among many brothers and sisters" (Romans 8:29 NIV). When we read the Bible and see Jesus, we are looking at the ultimate pattern and example for our lives.

Then Jesus went from Galilee to the Jordan River to be baptized by John. But John tried to talk him out of it. "I am the one who needs to be baptized by you," he said, "so why are you coming to me?"

But Jesus said, "It should be done, for we must carry out all that God requires." So John agreed to baptize him.

After his baptism, as Jesus came up out of the water, the heavens were opened and he saw the Spirit of God descending like a dove and settling on him. And a voice from heaven said, "This is my dearly loved Son, who brings me great joy" **(MATTHEW 3:13–17 NLT).**

Then the Spirit led Jesus into the desert to be tempted by the devil. Jesus fasted for forty days and nights. After this, he was very hungry. The devil came to Jesus to tempt him, saying, "If you are the Son of God, tell these rocks to become bread."

Jesus answered, "It is written in the Scriptures, 'A person lives not on bread alone, but by everything God says.'"

Then the devil led Jesus to the holy city of Jerusalem and put him on a high place of the Temple. The devil said, "If you are the Son of God, jump down, because it is written in the Scriptures:

> 'He has put his angels in charge of you. They will catch you in their hands so that you will not hit your foot on a rock.'"
> —Psalm 91:11–12

Jesus answered him, "It also says in the Scriptures, 'Do not test the Lord your God.'"

Then the devil led Jesus to the top of a very high mountain and showed him all the kingdoms of the world and all their splendor. The devil said, "If you will bow down and worship me, I will give you all these things."

Jesus said to the devil, "Go away from me, Satan! It is written in the Scriptures, 'You must worship the Lord your God and serve only him.'"

So the devil left Jesus, and angels came and took care of him. (MATTHEW 4:1-11 NCV)

At that time Jesus said, "I praise you, Father, Lord of heaven and earth, because you have hidden these things from the wise and learned, and revealed them to little children. Yes, Father, for this is what you were pleased to do.

All things have been committed to me by my Father. No one knows the Son except the Father, and no one knows the Father except the Son and those to whom the Son chooses to reveal him.

Come to me, all you who are weary and burdened, and I will give you rest. Take my yoke upon you and learn from me, for I am gentle and humble in heart, and you will find rest for your souls. For my yoke is easy and my burden is light" (MATTHEW 11:25-30 NIV).

Jesus, now well on the way up to Jerusalem, took the Twelve off to the side of the road and said, "Listen to me carefully. We are on our way up to Jerusalem. When we get there, the Son of Man will be betrayed to the religious leaders and scholars. They will sentence him to death. They will then hand him over to the Romans for mockery and torture and crucifixion. On the third day he will be raised up alive."

It was about that time that the mother of the Zebedee brothers came with her two sons and knelt before Jesus with a request.

"What do you want?" Jesus asked.

She said, "Give your word that these two sons of mine will be awarded the highest places of honor in your kingdom, one at your right hand, one at your left hand."

Jesus responded, "You have no idea what you're asking." And he said to James and John, "Are you capable of drinking the cup that I'm about to drink?"

They said, "Sure, why not?"

Jesus said, "Come to think of it, you are going to drink my cup. But as to awarding places of honor, that's not my business. My Father is taking care of that."

When the ten others heard about this, they lost their tempers, thoroughly disgusted with the two brothers. So Jesus got them together to settle things down. He said, "You've observed how godless rulers throw their weight around, how quickly a little power goes to their heads. It's not going to be that way with you. Whoever wants to be great must become a servant. Whoever wants to be first among you must be your slave. That is what the Son of Man has done: He came to serve, not be served—and then to give away his life in exchange for the many who are held hostage" (**MATTHEW 20:17–28 The Message**).

They went to the olive grove called Gethsemane, and Jesus said, "Sit here while I go and pray." He took Peter, James, and John with him, and he became deeply troubled and distressed. He told them, "My soul is crushed with grief to the point of death. Stay here and keep watch with me."

He went on a little farther and fell to the ground. He prayed that, if it were possible, the awful hour awaiting him might pass him by. "Abba, Father," he cried out, "everything is possible for you. Please take this cup of suffering away from me. Yet I want your will to be done, not mine."

Then he returned and found the disciples asleep. He said to Peter, "Simon, are you asleep? Couldn't you watch with me even one hour? Keep watch and pray, so that you will not give in to temptation. For the spirit is willing, but the body is weak."

Then Jesus left them again and prayed the same prayer as before. When he returned to them again, he found them sleeping, for they couldn't keep their eyes open. And they didn't know what to say.

When he returned to them the third time, he said, "Go ahead and sleep. Have your rest. But no—the time has come. The Son of Man is betrayed into the hands of sinners. Up, let's be going. Look, my betrayer is here!" (**MARK 14:32–42 NLT**)

Often we desire our heavenly Father to fix our problems and make them go away, but the example of Christ shows us that God's plan may be for us to go through difficulties.

Jesus said these things. Then, raising his eyes in prayer, he said: Father, it's time. Display the bright splendor of your Son so the Son in turn may show your bright splendor. You put him in charge of everything human so he might give real and eternal life to all in his charge. And this is the real and eternal life: That they know you, the one and only true God, and Jesus Christ, whom you sent. I glorified you on earth by completing down to the last detail what you assigned me to do. And now, Father, glorify me with your very own splendor, the very splendor I had in your presence before there was a world.

I spelled out your character in detail to the men and women you gave me. They were yours in the first place; then you gave them to me, and they have now done what you said. They know now, beyond the shadow of a doubt, that everything you gave me is firsthand from you, for the message you gave me, I gave them; and they took it, and were convinced that I came from you. They believed that you sent me. I pray for them. I'm not praying for the God-rejecting world but for those you gave me, for they are yours by right. Everything mine is yours, and yours mine, and my life is on display in them. For I'm no longer going to be visible in the world; they'll continue in the world while I return to you. Holy Father, guard them as they pursue this life that you conferred as a gift through me, so they can be one heart and mind as we are one heart and mind. As long as I was with them, I guarded them in the pursuit of the life you gave through me; I even posted a night watch. And not one of them got away, except for the rebel bent on destruction (the exception that proved the rule of Scripture).

Now I'm returning to you. I'm saying these things in the world's hearing so my people can experience my joy completed in them. I gave them your word; the godless world hated them because of it, because they didn't join the world's ways, just as I didn't join the world's ways. I'm not asking that you take them out of the world but that you guard them from the Evil One. They are no more defined by the world than I am defined by the world. Make them holy—consecrated—with the truth; your word is consecrating truth. In the same way that you gave me a mission in the world, I give them a mission in the world. I'm consecrating myself for their sakes so they'll be truth-consecrated in their mission.

I'm praying not only for them but also for those who will believe in me because of them and their witness about me. The goal is for all of them to become one heart and mind—just as you, Father, are in me and I in you, so they might be one heart and mind with us. Then the world might believe that you, in fact, sent me. The same glory you gave me, I gave them, so they'll be as unified and together as we are—I in them and you in me. Then they'll be mature in this oneness, and give the godless world evidence that you've sent me and loved them in the same way you've loved me. Father, I want those you gave me to be with me, right where I am, so they can see my glory, the splendor you gave me, having loved me long before there ever was a world. Righteous Father, the world has never known you, but I have known you, and these disciples know that you sent me on this mission. I have made your very being known to them—who you are and what you do—and continue to make it known, so that your love for me might be in them exactly as I am in them. (JOHN 17:1-26 THE MESSAGE)

For I consider that the sufferings of this present time are not worth comparing with the glory that is to be revealed to us. For the creation waits with eager longing for the revealing of the sons of God. For the creation was subjected to futility, not willingly, but because of him who subjected it, in hope that the creation itself will be set free from its bondage to corruption and obtain the freedom of the glory of the children of God. For we know that the whole creation has been groaning together in the pains of childbirth until now. And not only the creation, but we ourselves, who have the firstfruits of the Spirit, groan inwardly as we wait eagerly for adoption as sons, the redemption of our bodies. For in this hope we were saved. Now hope that is seen is not hope. For who hopes for what he sees? But if we hope for what we do not see, we wait for it with patience.

Likewise the Spirit helps us in our weakness. For we do not know what to pray for as we ought, but the Spirit himself intercedes for us with groanings too deep for words. And he who searches hearts knows what is the mind of the Spirit, because the Spirit intercedes for the saints according to the will of God. And we know that for those who love God all things work together for good, for those who are called according to his purpose. For those whom he foreknew he also predestined to be conformed to the image of his Son, in order that he might be the firstborn among many brothers. And those whom he predestined he also called, and those whom he called he also justified, and those whom he justified he also glorified. **(ROMANS 8:18-30 ESV)**

Now we who are strong ought to bear the weaknesses of those without strength and not just please ourselves. Each of us is to please his neighbor for his good, to his edification. For even Christ did not please Himself; but as it is written, "The reproaches of those who reproached You fell on Me." For whatever was written in earlier times was written for our instruction, so that through perseverance and the encouragement of the Scriptures we might have hope. Now may the God who gives perseverance and encouragement grant you to be of the same mind with one another according to Christ Jesus, so that with one accord you may with one voice glorify the God and Father of our Lord Jesus Christ. Therefore, accept one another, just as Christ also accepted us to the glory of God. **(ROMANS 15:1-7 NASB)**

But just as you abound in everything, in faith and utterance and knowledge and in all earnestness and in the love we inspired in you, see that you abound in this gracious work also. I am not speaking this as a command, but as proving through the earnestness of others the sincerity of your love also. For you know the grace of our Lord Jesus Christ, that though He was rich, yet for your sake He became poor, so that you through His poverty might become rich. **(2 CORINTHIANS 8:7-9 NASB)**

It is the same for us. We were once like children, slaves to the useless rules of this world. But when the right time came, God sent his Son who was born of a woman and lived under the law. God did this so he could buy freedom for those who were under the law and so we could become his children. (GALATIANS 4:3–5)

Christ was more than just an example of a perfect big brother—he purchased salvation for all of God's family.

Remember that in the past you were without Christ. You were not citizens of Israel, and you had no part in the agreements with the promise that God made to his people. You had no hope, and you did not know God. But now in Christ Jesus, you who were far away from God are brought near through the blood of Christ's death. Christ himself is our peace. He made both Jewish people and those who are not Jews one people. They were separated as if there were a wall between them, but Christ broke down that wall of hate by giving his own body. The Jewish law had many commands and rules, but Christ ended that law. His purpose was to make the two groups of people become one new people in him and in this way make peace. It was also Christ's purpose to end the hatred between the two groups, to make them into one body, and to bring them back to God. Christ did all this with his death on the cross. Christ came and preached peace to you who were far away from God, and to those who were near to God. Yes, it is through Christ we all have the right to come to the Father in one Spirit. (EPHESIANS 2:12–18 NCV)

Do not be interested only in your own life, but be interested in the lives of others. In your lives you must think and act like Christ Jesus. Christ himself was like God in everything. But he did not think that being equal with God was something to be used for his own benefit. But he gave up his place with God and made himself nothing. He was born to be a man and became like a servant. And when he was living as a man, he humbled himself and was fully obedient to God, even when that caused his death—death on a cross. So God raised him to the highest place. God made his name greater than every other name so that every knee will bow to the name of Jesus—everyone in heaven, on earth, and under the earth. And everyone will confess that Jesus Christ is Lord and bring glory to God the Father. **(PHILIPPIANS 2:4–11 NCV)**

Therefore, since we have a great high priest who has passed through the heavens, Jesus the Son of God, let us hold fast our confession. For we do not have a high priest who cannot sympathize with our weaknesses, but One who has been tempted in all things as we are, yet without sin. Therefore let us draw near with confidence to the throne of grace, so that we may receive mercy and find grace to help in time of need. **(HEBREWS 4:14–16 NASB)**

For to this you have been called, because Christ also suffered for you, leaving you an example, so that you might follow in his steps. He committed no sin, neither was deceit found in his mouth. When he was reviled, he did not revile in return; when he suffered, he did not threaten, but continued entrusting himself to him who judges justly. He himself bore our sins in his body on the tree, that we might die to sin and live to righteousness. By his wounds you have been healed. For you were straying like sheep, but have now returned to the Shepherd and Overseer of your souls. **(1 PETER 2:21–25 ESV)**

See how very much our Father loves us, for he calls us his children, and that is what we are! But the people who belong to this world don't recognize that we are God's children because they don't know him. Dear friends, we are already God's children, but he has not yet shown us what we will be like when Christ appears. But we do know that we will be like him, for we will see him as he really is. And all who have this eager expectation will keep themselves pure, just as he is pure.

Everyone who sins is breaking God's law, for all sin is contrary to the law of God. And you know that Jesus came to take away our sins, and there is no sin in him. Anyone who continues to live in him will not sin. But anyone who keeps on sinning does not know him or understood who he is. (1 JOHN 3:1-6 NLT)

For this is the message that you heard from the beginning, that we should love one another, not as Cain who was of the wicked one and murdered his brother. And why did he murder him? Because his works were evil and his brother's righteous.

Do not marvel, my brethren, if the world hates you. We know that we have passed from death to life, because we love the brethren. He who does not love his brother abides in death. Whoever hates his brother is a murderer, and you know that no murderer has eternal life abiding in him.

By this we know love, because He laid down His life for us. And we also ought to lay down our lives for the brethren. But whoever has this world's goods, and sees his brother in need, and shuts up his heart from him, how does the love of God abide in him?

My little children, let us not love in word or in tongue, but in deed and in truth. And by this we know that we are of the truth, and shall assure our hearts before Him. For if our heart condemns us, God is greater than our heart, and knows all things. Beloved, if our heart does not condemn us, we have confidence toward God. And whatever we ask we receive from Him, because we keep His commandments and do those things that are pleasing in His sight. And this is His commandment: that we should believe on the name of His Son Jesus Christ and love one another, as He gave us commandment.

Now he who keeps His commandments abides in Him, and He in him. And by this we know that He abides in us, by the Spirit whom He has given us. **(1 JOHN 3:11–24 NKJV)**

Notes

Introduction

1. Bill Cosby, *Fatherhood* (New York: Peter Pauper Press, 2002), 18.
2. George W. Holden, *Parenting: A Dynamic Perspective* (Los Angeles: SAGE, 2009), 28.

Chapter 1: What God Expects From Parents

3. C. H. Spurgeon, *John Ploughman's Talk and Pictures, Or Plain Advice for Plain People* (Philadelphia: Henry Altemus, 1896), 150.

Chapter 2: How Parents Affect Their Children

4. C. S. Lewis, The Four Loves (New York: Harcourt Brace, 1963), 42.

Chapter 3: What God Expects From Children

5. Bill Cosby, *Fatherhood* (New York: Peter Pauper Press, 2002), 18.

Chapter 4: How Children's Behavior Affects Their Parents . . . and Their Own Future

6. Anne Frank, Harry Paape, David Barnouw, Gerrold van der Stroom, trans., Arnold Pomerans, B. M. Mooyaart-Doubleday, Susan Massotty, *The Diary of Anne Frank: The Revised Critical Edition* (New York: Doubleday, 2003), 711–712.

Chapter 5: Sons and Daughters in Particular

7. Edward T. Imparato, *General MacArthur: Speeches and Reports 1908–1964* (Paducah, KY: Turner Publishing, 2000), 127.

8. Michael K. Deaver, *A Different Drummer: My Thirty Years With Ronald Reagan* (New York: HarperCollins, 2001), 37.

Chapter 6: Children and Miracles

9. Greg. S. Kessler, *Internet Wisdom: The Book* (Bloomington, IN: Author-House, 2007), 171.

Chapter 7: Children and Faith

10. Jonathan Edwards, *Religious Affections* (New Haven: Yale University Press, 1959), 118.

Chapter 8: God, the Perfect Father

11. Kent Nerburn, *Letters to My Son: A Father's Wisdom on Manhood, Women, Life and Love* (Oakland, CA: New World Library, 1994), chap. 25.

Chapter 9: Jesus, the Perfect Son

12. Tyron Edwards, *A Dictionary of Thoughts: Being a Cyclopedia of Laconic Quotations From the Best Authors of the World, Both Ancient and Modern* (Detroit, MI: F. B. Dickerson Co, 1906), 583.

More Insight from God's Word

Countless books have been written about how to pray, but this book includes exactly what *God* says about prayer. This one-stop resource organizes every prayer and primary reference to prayer in the Bible and includes brief, accessible commentaries for even more insight.

Everything the Bible Says About Prayer

Have you ever wanted to ask God what heaven is like? It turns out, he's already told us! The Bible is filled with passages that describe it. In this book, you will find all the scriptural references to heaven, as well as brief, clear explanations from trustworthy commentaries.

Everything the Bible Says About Heaven

How people deal with money matters to God. In this short volume, all the scriptural references to money have been collected and explained in a clear and concise format. Hear what God has to say about everything related to money, including working, saving, tithing—and more!

Everything the Bible Says About Money

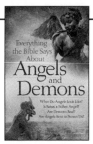

Supernatural beings—both the good and bad—fascinate us because they are surrounded by mystery. This book includes every Scripture passage relating to angels and demons, along with brief commentaries to help you develop a clear, biblical point of view.

Everything the Bible Says About Angels and Demons

◊ BETHANYHOUSE